The Museum of Modern Art,
Saint-Etienne

Open daily from 10 a.m. to 7 p.m.
(Wednesday: 8 p.m.), except Tuesday
La Terrasse
42000 Saint-Etienne
Tel.: 77 93 59 58

MUSÉES ET MONUMENTS DE FRANCE
PUBLISHED WITH THE SUPPORT OF THE FONDATION PARIBAS
COLLECTION DIRECTED BY PIERRE LEMOINE

THE MUSEUM OF MODERN ART
SAINT-ÉTIENNE

JACQUES BEAUFFET
BERNARD CEYSSON
MARTINE DANCER
MAURICE FRÉCHURET

MUSÉES ET MONUMENTS DE FRANCE
CITY OF SAINT-ÉTIENNE & ALBIN MICHEL

The collection Musées et
Monuments de France has
been created on the initiative of
the Fondation Paribas

Cover:
Fernand Léger
Argentan 1881 - Gif-sur-Yvette 1955
Three Women against Red Background,
1927 (detail)
Purchased in 1983. Inv. 83.14.1A

Frontispiece:
Claude Viallat (Nîmes 1936)
Painting, 1978
Paint on patched canvas; 380 x 295
Purchased in 1979. Inv. 79.34.1

This volume is dedicated to all those who have contributed in
one way or another to the expansion of the collection of
modern and contemporary art of the Museum since the
acquisition of Monet's *Water-Lilies* study: the donators, the
successive municipalities, the Direction des Musées de
France, the Fonds Régional d'Acquisition des Musées, the
Fonds National d'Art Contemporain, and the Fonds Régional
d'Art Contemporain Rhône-Alpes.
However, this collection would never have existed, were it
not for the ardour and obstinacy of Maurice Allemand.
Similarly, this publication would not have been possible
without a generous patronage, stimulating the Museum's
activities and above all the growth of its collection.
For all the gratitude we owe to *Casino* for an exemplary
partnership, it is to Antoine Guichard that we are most
indebted for his offering the opportunity to present at
Saint-Etienne one of the great European collections of the
art of our century.
BERNARD CEYSSON, JACQUES BEAUFFET

Introduction

At the start of the nineteenth century, Saint-Etienne, though an industrious and prosperous settlement, was no more than a large village, with no great tradition or history. It had not yet achieved the status of departmental capital and was therefore not the beneficiary, as were the chief cities of France, of the state loans that formed the basis of the officially listed museums. It was the donation, by an *honnête homme* or gentleman named Eyssautier, of a collection of curios assembled to instruct the young people of the working class that led to the creation of a museum. Initially lodged in the Hôtel de Ville or town hall, the collection was transferred to the Palais des Arts during the second half of the century, and, under its later name of Musée d'Art et d'Industrie (Museum of Art and Industry), it underwent rapid expansion following the appointment of Marius Vachon as its curator. Although Vachon's period of office was all too brief, it marked the real beginning of the history of the museums of Saint-Etienne—or rather of the Musée d'Art et d'Industrie, of which the present Musée d'Art Moderne (Museum of Modern Art), Musée d'Art et d'Industrie (currently being renovated), and Musée de la Mine (Museum of Mining; now under development) are in fact merely extensions; they are all departments of Vachon's remarkable original museographical project, progressive and modernist in its outlook. The invitation extended to Vachon by the elected representatives of Saint-Etienne to take charge of the town's youthful museum was not the result of chance or good connections. Vachon, an 'Inspecteur des Beaux-Arts', had won some acclaim for his investigations into industrial art in Germany and Austria. In the course of these, he had become aware of the degree to which France lagged behind in this field, and he had envisaged museums as training centres to be used to prepare the way for the revival of the French craft industry and its 'industrialization'. Given that they faced a grave crisis heralding the decline of the arms and ribbon industries of Saint-Etienne, it is easy to see why the town's businessmen and councillors should have turned to Vachon. In fact, however, it rapidly became obvious that Vachon's ideas ran completely counter to the implicit intentions of the notables of Saint-Etienne. They believed that by creating a museum and setting the recent past in a sort of 'mythical' eternity, they would be able to recapture their lost prosperity. The councillors' aim was to ward off misfortune, whereas Marius

Vachon, who had little desire to glorify what had disappeared, envisaged the Museum as a training and information centre, with the character not so much of a treasure-house as of a repository of objects available for study. To the collections of arms and ribbons already envisaged, and which he set about expanding, Vachon planned to add a library and photographic collection, and a collection of paintings and sculptures intended to provide armourers, arms engravers, designers, and makers of passementerie or trimmings with paradigms of 'The Beautiful'. The Museum as Vachon conceived it was a veritable people's university, a forerunner, in its time and in its own way, of the Bauhaus. As such, it was inevitable that it should clash with the ideas and customs of a rather timid group of people, whose greatest fear was the emergence of an enlightened and well-informed working class. As a result, Vachon's scheme was rapidly abandoned.

Following Vachon's departure, and particularly in the inter-war years, the Museum experienced its gloomiest moments. At the end of the nineteenth century and the beginning of twentieth, however, the Bancel and Ogier bequests had enabled the foundations of a fine collection of paintings, sculptures, and other artefacts to be laid, even though it was, it must be said, a collection befitting a good 'connoisseur' rather than a museum. A number of rather fortunate purchases, including that of an excellent *Water-Lilies* study from Claude Monet himself, had enhanced the collection. But such acquisitions were all too few in number. In 1934—a fateful date—the Fine Arts Commission elected to use funds from the bequest that had financed the purchase of the Monet to buy paintings on rustic themes by Balande and Girardin—despite the fact that some of its members had their eye on a Bonnard or a Matisse. These rustic works heralded the wave of nostalgia that was to transport a large section of French society to the lamentable ideological realms of the 'back to the land' movement. During these years, Saint-Etienne, sadly, did not display the bold opening-up to contemporary art practised in Grenoble. And yet the town might well have accepted such an approach. Despite the consternation and surprise he caused following his appointment as curator of the Museum in 1947, Maurice Allemand nevertheless won acceptance. The twenty years he devoted to the Museum deserve greater consideration than the few lines accorded them here—they were twenty years of adventure, illustrative of the history of relations between French provincial museums and modern art. As Andry-Farcy before him at Grenoble, Maurice Allemand wrote his own particular page in that history, at a time when most of his peers showed themselves indifferent, if not hostile, to one of the finest portions of the French heritage. The achievements of Maurice Allemand obviously include the opening-up of the Museum to modern art, but he must also be credited with enriching the 'old' collection by the addition of several major works. By means either of municipally funded purchases or of State acquisitions which he suggested in order to secure their loan for Saint-Etienne, or again by the donations he managed to elicit, Maurice Allemand brought into the collection works by, amongst others, Villon, Severini, Gleizes, Zadkine, Matisse, Bryen, Arp, Calder, Bram Van Velde, Vasarely, Etienne Martin, and Cardenas. In 1968, at a time when Russian and Soviet art were not yet in vogue, it was Allemand who urged me to buy the small painting on wood by Kudriachov now in the Museum's collection.

Post-war France showed little grasp of developments in modern art,

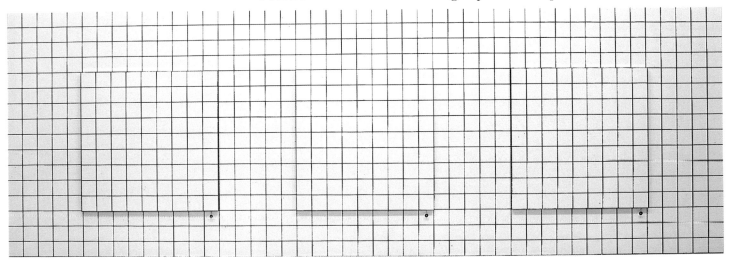

Jean-Pierre Raynaud (Colombes 1939)
Zero Space, 1987
White tiling, black jointing, metal numbers and frames; 355 x 1045 x 7
Commissioned, 1987. Inv. 88.8.1

despite the fact that it had originated on French soil, and Maurice Allemand, like the majority of his colleagues in the provinces at that time, did not have extensive funds for acquisitions. One of his merits was to have managed, despite his penury, to organize some of the first great exhibitions in France devoted to the history of twentieth-century art. The 1957 exhibition, which provided a panorama of the sources of abstract art, made an indelible impression on all those who had the good fortune to see it. Given the present state of the market, such an exhibition would not be feasible today, and it is difficult for us to appreciate just how bold and breathtaking it was. To a public totally uninformed in regard to twentieth-century art, it offered a captivating panorama of the sources of abstract art, pointing to its international character and thus revealing to most of those who visited it that Paris had not been the only active centre of modernist artistic creativity. This masterly display was to be followed by other events of similar breadth, the best-known of which—and justifiably so—demonstrated the importance of collage and assemblage in twentieth-century art. This event of 1964 saw the exhibition, probably for the first time in a French museum, of works by Rauschenberg, Jim Dine, and others.

Since 1967 we have been simultaneously pursuing the plans of both Maurice Allemand and Marius Vachon, attempting to translate the latter's ideas into reality in a way that takes account of developments in Saint-Etienne, in its industry, and, of course, in art itself—developments which Vachon could not have foreseen. Thanks to increases in funds for acquisitions granted by the municipal authorities, central government, the regional authorities, and, since 1987, the Casino sponsorship, we have been able to expand the collection and, following in the tracks of Maurice Allemand, transform it into one of the richest public collections of contemporary art in France. Its scope and quality will be revealed to readers as they turn the pages of this book.

At the end of the 1970s, the collection began to seem somewhat cramped. The Musée d'Art et d'Industrie was now too small to allow

Alexander Calder
Philadelphia 1898 - New York 1976
Three Wings, 1963
Stabile, metal painted black;
approx. 300 x 300 x 300
Deposited by the National Museum
of Modern Art, 1985

the requisite standard of presentation. The idea of an extension or new building, purpose-built for the display of works of modern and contemporary art, had been circulating for some years. In 1981, work was begun on a draft schedule, and by 1982 the basic outline of the project had been determined and was given concrete shape by Didier Guichard. It was originally intended to locate the building on the site of the Couriot mine-shaft, disarmed in 1973 and situated within the town, 500 metres from the centre. The intention—seemingly practical, but in fact highly symbolic—was to combine tradition (the collection of arms, ribbons, and cycles) with innovation (modern and contemporary art) in a celebration of the history of mining. However, intractable problems of access very soon became evident on this site, and the question of the dust was also—dare I say it—raised. This was dust carried into the site offices set up in the surface buildings of the Couriot shaft by northerly and westerly winds blowing off the slag-heaps; papers, books, files, and furniture were covered in a thick layer of black dust. There could be no thought of subjecting the Museum's works of art to such an onslaught. In 1983, François Dubanchet proposed that the Museum of Modern Art be built to the north of the town, on the spot named 'la Doa', which he judged more convenient and more suitable. This judicious decision again had a symbolic value. And Didier Guichard fully grasped this: he opened the Museum up to the north, towards level country and areas that bear little trace of the now-closed industrial chapter of the region's history; but at the same time he used the brilliant black ceramic shield in which he encased the Museum as a reminder that coal was once extracted from an open-cast mine on this site. In January 1986, after the inevitable ups and downs that mark the course of any project between its conception and the start of work, the first stone was laid; the keys were handed over in September 1987; and the Museum was officially opened on 10 December of the same year.

The architectural line taken by Didier Guichard was a simple one: he aimed, not to create one of those monuments to the glory of the architect that one sometimes encounters, and thus to display the remarkable and distinctive features of his genius, but, on the contrary, to produce a sober building, resolutely functional and at the service of the works it housed. The cost of the project had to be kept low and was fixed at the outset, when the scheme was first set in motion. And these commitments were fulfilled. The architect and his team, and the Museum's management had to bear in mind the risk which the municipal authorities had taken—not without some courage—at a time of economic constraint. Working against the prevailing postmodernist trend, Didier Guichard opted for a design that is simple in form: an external structure of 'minimal'-style blocks, and, internally, a series of neutral spaces, harmoniously proportioned and arranged along right-angled grid-lines. White walls, grey flooring, and a precise mix of natural and artificial light, filtered through an unobtrusive mechanism allowing great flexibility in lighting, combine with the structural simplicity of the building to produce a tranquil 'abode', suffused in an even light that allows the exhibits to put their message across without ostentation.

Having said all this, we should make it clear that the Museum of Modern Art does more than just host exhibitions. It serves the community as an educational centre, organizing courses and talks, and putting on workshops and other activities linked to the collections or to the exhibitions. It also houses a library providing students and researchers with a source of material on twentieth-century art that is unrivalled in quality, being the only one of its kind outside Paris. Finally, working closely with the University, and in particular with the Centre d'Etudes et de Recherche sur l'Expression Contemporaine, the Museum functions as a centre for scholarly research. Five of the seminars organized in this connection have produced follow-up publications. The Museum thus aims to fulfil a twofold objective: to bring together a collection of works of international renown, and to take part in the life of the city, of which it is, without doubt, one of the jewels.

BERNARD CEYSSON   Director of the Museum

Modern Art

The Museum's collection of paintings and sculptures from the first half of this century was assembled at a late date. With the exception of the bold acquisition of the Monet *Water-Lilies* tondo at the beginning of the 1920s, it was not until the start of the 1950s that the first significant components of a systematic collection of twentieth-century art were recorded in the Museum's inventories. However, Maurice Allemand had busied himself elsewhere—and with considerable success— expanding a collection of 'old' paintings, the importance and quality of which his predecessors had failed to discern. At a time when Grenoble was the only museum—or practically the only one—outside Paris to pay any attention to twentieth-century art, the ignorance, not to say hostility, of the public made the acquisition of such works at Saint-Etienne arduous; all the more so since funds for acquisition were meagre after the war (priority being given to reconstruction and the restoration of the country's system of production) and remained so until the start of the 1970s. Nevertheless, thanks to donations elicited through a programme of exhibitions unequalled in France, and thanks also to various State deposits and a number of judicious purchases, Maurice Allemand was able to bring together a number of works typifying the great movements of the beginnings of modern art, notably works by Matisse, Severini, Marcoussis, Zadkine, Gleizes, Csaky, Villon, Kudriachov, Freundlich, Beothy, Arp, and Calder. A number of factors have enabled us to continue the process of collecting begun by Maurice Allemand, without as a result having to limit our planned purchases of works from the second half of the century: from 1972, the municipal authorities, determined to transform the Museum of Art and Industry into a major museum of modern art, agreed appropriate funding, greatly increasing this throughout the 1980s; these funds were supplemented by regular—immensely valuable—grants from central government and the regional authorities (FRAM); assistance was also received from the Fonds du Patrimoine. As a result, the Museum was able to acquire works by Picabia, Schwitters, Raoul Hausmann, Magnelli, Aleksandra Exter, Masson, Hélion, and others. However, it was the entry into the collection, in 1983, of Fernand Léger's *Three Women against Red Background* (1927) that really marked the beginning of the expansion of this part of the collection. The acquisition of this work, formerly part of a renowned Belgian collection, resulted from the happy concert of local and central government. Shortly

Alberto Magnelli
Florence 1888 - Paris 1971
Lyrical Explosion No. 19, 1918
Oil on canvas; 140 x 93
Purchased, 1986. Inv. 86.14.1

11

after this, the collection was further enhanced by the deposit of works of art from the National Museum of Modern Art, including a number of items acquired for the State by dation. The Museum thus acquired two further works by Léger, a late but important Miró, a monumental stabile by Calder, a key 1930s painting by Kandinsky, a historic work by Francis Gruber, and other items which meant that it was able to give a proper account of the major trends in art in the first half of this century. Some important donations enhanced this panorama yet further, adding works by Magnelli and Hélion, and an impressive set of paintings and drawings by Victor Brauner. Various fortunate purchases (Herbin, Tanguy, Duchamp, Domela, etc.) complemented the collection. What seemed impossible twenty years ago has become a reality. Though not able to claim equal standing with collections such as those of Grenoble or Villeneuve-d'Ascq, the works brought together in the Museum of Modern Art at Saint-Etienne nevertheless constitute an excellent introduction—comprising many masterpieces—to what forms the heart of its collection: art from the 1950s to the present day.   B.C.

The Beginnings
If in France at the beginning of the twentieth century, Impressionism was still an avant-garde movement, Gauguin, Cézanne, and Van Gogh had already emerged as the figureheads of a mythology to which Nabis, Fauves, and Cubists would later refer, in line with their different aims and rejecting the notion that everything must be subordinated exclusively to visual impressions.

In the *Citadel at Belle-Ile* of 1896, Matisse is taking the first steps on the path leading to extravagances of colour which Louis Vauxcelles would describe as 'fauves' (like wild beasts) at the Salon d'Automne of 1905. Matisse had discovered light, and was beginning to express himself through colour. The paint is applied thickly, like cladding on a wall, but it is still restrained in comparison with the vividness of Chabaud's *Red Nude*.

Felix Vallotton belonged to the circle of Nabis grouped, in about 1888, around Sérusier and his painting *The Talisman*, executed under direct instruction from Gauguin. In his *Nude* of 1924, Vallotton attempts a sculptural transcription on to canvas of a young semi-nude female model.

The writings of the Nabi 'elder' Maurice Denis earned him a certain regard amongst his younger colleagues. In 1907, completely absorbed in his Christian preoccupations, he attempted, with works like *The Communicants*, to recapture the atmosphere of mystery and legend such as prevails in the works of Fra Angelico.

In *The Gate of Hell*, Rodin embarked on a gigantic work in which, following in the footsteps of Dante and inspired by Baudelaire, he brought together all the great sufferings and tragedies of history. Camille Claudel was probably the model for the *Danaïd*. Rodin, donning the mantle of the visionary, distances himself from literal representation in his attempt to express the exhaustion and utter anguish of the body, voluptuously gathered up. This work was exhibited with

August Chabaud
Nîmes 1882 - Graveson 1955
Red Nude, 1905
Oil on cardboard; 105 x 75
Deposited by the State, 1954
Inv. D.54.2.5

Claude Monet
Paris 1840 - Giverny 1926
Water-Lilies, 1907
Oil on canvas. Diameter: 90
Purchased, 1926. Anc. inv. F.398

Auguste Rodin
(Paris 1840 - Meudon 1917)
Danaïd, 1885
Bronze; 32 x 64 x 46
Deposited by the Musée du Louvre
Inv. D.13.1.47

Maurice Denis
Granville 1870 - Paris 1943
The Communicants, 1907
Oil on canvas; 98 x 107.2
Purchased, 1972. Inv. 72.9.1

František Kupka
Opocno 1871 - Puteaux 1957
The Blue Ribbon, 1910
Oil on canvas; 65 x 71
Deposited by the National Museum
of Modern Art, 1966. Inv. D.66.4.1

Monet's *Water-Lilies* at the 1907 exhibition in the Georges Petit Gallery.

The *Water-Lilies*, bought from Monet himself in 1925, no longer fall within the ambit of Impressionism. In 1907, Monet laid the foundations of a new pictorial concept heralding the American 'all over' colourfield. His water-lily garden at Giverny, and the works of the Japanese artist Hiroshige, to which he constantly referred, are the sources for this landscape from which all allusion to space is banished. The reflections from the water, the lilies, and the play of light are all that fills the canvas, with its distinctive tondo shape. 'These

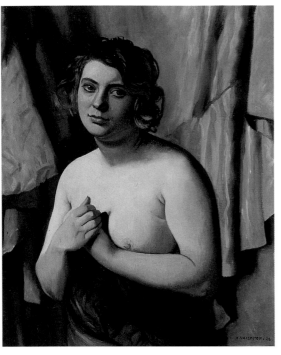

Félix Vallotton
Lausanne 1865 - Paris 1929
Semi-Nude Woman, 1924
Oil on canvas; 81.2 x 65
Deposited by the State, 1986

Henri Matisse
Le Cateau 1869 - Nice 1954
The Citadel at Belle-Ile, 1896
Oil on canvas; 32.8 x 40.8
Purchased, 1966. Inv. 66.2.1

Albert Gleizes
Paris 1881 - Avignon 1953
Painting with Seven Elements
Oil on canvas; 216.4 x 181.5
Deposited by the National Museum of
Modern Art, 1986. Inv. D.86.1.3

landscapes of light and water', said Monet, 'have become an obsession', a search to express what he feels.

In 1907, Chabaud, for his part, spatters his feelings across canvases that are full of fire and discord. Arbitrary in his choice of colour, swift in his execution, and lacking in respect for decreed artistic rules, Chabaud has a style of expression in the tradition of the Fauves, and in particular of Van Dongen, with whom he shared an interest in Parisian life. In his *Blue Ribbon* of 1910, Frantisek Kupka demonstrates the transition of 1910-12 from liberated, subjective expression to the first attempts to forgo representation. The woman in this painting, with her green-shaded purple face, is encircled by a succession of sculpted brushstrokes that look more like a collection of coloured planes than a landscape. Kupka is opening a new chapter in the history of painting.   M.D.

Cubism and its Associates From 1908, Braque and Picasso began to tackle the rules governing the internal organization of paintings, dismantling reality in order to capture its multiple facets, and attempting to create a more objective image than that offered by straightforward appearance. Gleizes, La Fresnaye, Marcoussis, and others all felt that they were defending a common aesthetic, labelled 'Cubism'

Julio González
Barcelona 1876 - Arcueil 1942
Dancer with Daisy
Bronze; approx. 33 x 10
Deposited by the National Museum of
Modern Art, 1986. Inv. D.86.1.5

Henri Laurens
Paris 1885 - Paris 1954
Small Seated Woman, 1932
Bronze (lost wax); 34 x 26.5 x 18
Deposited by the National Museum
of Modern Art, 1974. Inv. D.74.2.1

by the critics. In Italy in 1909, Marinetti unleashed the watchwords of Italian futurism: 'love of danger', 'daring and rebellion', 'the beauty of speed'. The Futurist Severini came to France and discovered in the Cubist style of expression a corroboration of the overwrought desire for modernism. Thus *Still Life with Lacerba* (1913) is reminiscent of the papiers collés used by Braque and Picasso to 'give proof of realism by putting the object in the picture'. The papier collé, though a representational element, also introduces a concrete reality into the work: the 'Lacerba' of Severini's picture is a fragment of the Futurist periodical of that name. Still life, which is a concentration on common, everyday objects, has often been chosen as a theme because time and the anecdotal can be excluded from it, and attention focused exclusively on the plastic beauty of the motifs. La Fresnaye and Marcoussis confirm the lasting nature of this genre. During the Second World War, Picasso too was to create anew the banal spectacle

Pablo Picasso
Malaga 1881 - Mougins 1973
Still Life with Cherries, 1943
Oil on canvas; 53.9 x 80.9
Deposited by the National Museum
of Modern Art, 1984. Inv. D.84.3.5

Louis Marcoussis
Warsaw 1883 - Cusset (Allier), 1941
Still Life with Jug, 1925
Oil on canvas; 33 x 41
Purchased, 1955. Inv. 55.4.1

of reality, an attempt which, given the restrictions then prevailing, assumed new meaning. He demonstrated his resistance by using a form of expression outlawed by the occupying forces.

In Russia, Futurism, Cubism, and the lessons of Matisse were being developed and extended by a dynamic avant-garde. In *Landscape with Houses* of 1911, Aleksandra Exter, who embodies the links between France, Italy, and Russia, marries together Cubist and Futurist languages. In Kudriachov's 1919 *Composition*, the 'Bundles of Energy that Traverse the Universe' are transcribed on to canvas in a gamut of grey tones.

Gino Severini
Cortone 1883 - Meudon 1966
Still Life with Periodical Lacerba, c. 1913-16
Papiers collés, Indian ink, pencil,
charcoal, gouache and chalk; 50 x 66
Deposited by the State, 1956
Inv. D.56.4.1

Sculpture too was reflecting on its aims, given the new means at its disposal. Csaky's bronze *Cubist Head* of 1914, and Zadkine's 1920 *Woman with Fan* betray the initial influence of Cubist methods, but these artists were later to move away from such methods, as was Henri Laurens, whose 1932 *Small Seated Woman* documents a simplification and suppling of forms. Julio González opened up a new area of artistic activity by using ironwork in sculpture, welding together basic iron components. In his *Dancer with Daisy* (1937-38) he 'traces in the air' a silhouette vibrant with life.

In 1921, after a period of theoretical endeavour during

Ossip Zadkine
Smolensk 1890 - Paris 1967
Woman with Fan, 1920
Pouillenay stone; 86.5 x 33 x 25
Purchased, 1960. Inv. 60.3.1

Joseph Csaky
Szeged (Hungary) 1888 - Paris 1971
Cubist Head, 1914
Bronze; 38.5 x 21.5 x 21.5
Deposited by the State, 1959
Inv. D.59.4.7

Pablo Picasso
Malaga 1881 - Mougins 1973
Still Life: Jug, Glass, and Orange, 1944
Oil on canvas; 33 x 41
Given by the artist, 1944. Inv. 44.2.1

Pablo Picasso
Malaga 1881 - Mougins 1973
Provençal Borage, 1952
Ceramic (single piece); 61.5 x 26 x 40
Given by the artist, 1953. Inv. 53.6.1

which, with Metzinger, he published *Du Cubisme* (1912), Albert Gleizes turned along a different path. In an attempt to introduce rhythm into his 'tableau objet' *Painting with Seven Elements* (1924-34), he links the various components with cadenced patterns and circles. Gleizes was attracted by the ideals of communal life, and he belongs to the tradition of those who sought to renew their links with certain types of skilled handicrafts. In this context of a resurgence of handicraft traditions, which began in 1946, Picasso turned to ceramics, either creating entirely new objects or using existing ones as a basis for his work. One example is *Provençal Borage*

(1952), in which the volume of the female figure is created by allusion, by the curve of the handle transformed into woman's hair. M.D.

Léger In 1983, the concerted efforts of central government and the municipal authorities made possible the entry into the Museum's collections of an important work by Fernand Léger: *Three Women against Red Background*, painted in 1927 and formerly part of a renowned Belgian collection. This painting, which may be considered one of the artist's major works, is undoubtedly one of the masterpieces of the twentieth century. It may be likened to two other paintings, but, although all three depict female figures against a red background—one, two, and three figures respectively—they do not form a series. The paintings concerned are: *Nude against Red Background*, which was also executed in 1927 and, having formerly been part of the Cuttoli Collection, is now owned by the Hirshhorn Museum, Washington; and *Two Nudes against Red Background*, owned by the Museum of Basle and painted in 1923. A drawing in the Masurel Collection which establishes the motifs and hieratic frontality of the Saint-Etienne painting suggests that the work was conceived in that year—whether before or after the Basle painting, is an open question. The drawing concerned could equally well

Roger de La Fresnaye
Le Mans 1885 - Grasse 1925
Still Life with Tea Pot, 1912
Oil on canvas; 46 x 55
Deposited by the National Museum
of Modern Art, 1986. Inv. D.86.1.2

Ivan Kudriachov
Kaluga 1896 - Moscow 1972
Composition, 1919
Oil on wooden panel; 47 x 40.5
Purchased, 1971. Inv. 71.1.1

Aleksandra Exter
Kiev 1882 - Paris 1949
Landscape with Houses, 1911
Oil on canvas; 82 x 65
Purchased, 1973. Inv. 73.6.1

23

Fernand Léger
Argentan 1881 - Gif-sur-Yvette 1955
Three Women against Red Background, 1927
Oil on canvas; 140 x 96
Purchased, 1983. Inv. 83.14.1A

have served as a preliminary sketch for another of Léger's paintings, executed the following year, namely *Three Figures*, which make an interesting comparison with *Three Women against Red Background*. Most of the works of this period display a common concern to achieve monumentality, evident in the emphatic black contours that accentuate the robust geometry of the masses and volumes. In a more forceful manner than in *Le Grand Déjeuner* (1921), and indeed than in *La Lecture* (1924), Léger here provides us with a splendid statement of 'the need to follow up the dynamism of the "mechanical period" with the staticness of his "large-scale figures"' (on this, see the monograph by G. Bauquier). After the war, Léger followed Picasso and others in returning to a classicism beyond which the pre-1914 'experiments' had not really moved, and with which they actually never intended to break completely. The various nudes against red background, like many paintings of the period, contain allusions—as Christopher Green has amply demonstrated—to Roman mosaic art, as discussed in an article in *L'Esprit Nouveau*. It is therefore not by chance that Léger, with his uncluttered, 'mechanical' organization of forms, sets ancient sources within the framework of the 'radiant' modernity to which Le Corbusier and Ozenfant wish to pledge humanity. Yet Léger, an admirer of Charlie Chaplin, was fearful of the dehumanization implied by a perfect order, and, although tempted towards a rigorous and decorative style of geometric abstraction, he quickly overcame this bent. The small 1929 still life deposited at Saint-Etienne by the National Museum of Modern Art does, however, still show traces of that pull, in its strong, slightly Art Deco stylization.

After the Second World War, Léger achieved a kind of synthesis of his art and beliefs. The classicism of the 1920s was finally made to serve deliberately popular themes. The common people, whose simplicity and linguistic inventiveness Léger had discovered in the trenches of the Great War, were confirmed, with great force, in their roles as the builders of the future. Léger also painted their leisure pursuits: *The Country Outing* of 1953 (second version, deposited by the National Museum of Modern Art) is Manet's *Déjeuner sur l'herbe* but impregnated with the poetry of Jean Renoir. Only modern art could have produced this limpid and sunny heroization of the myths of the Front Populaire; and only Fernand Léger could have achieved it with such lyricism and simplicity. The subject is drawn from Impressionism; the order of composition from Cubism; and the sharply outlined spreads of colour from Fauvism. Léger's delight in pure colour, in primary colours intensified by black contours, recalls the art of Mondrian. But Léger rejects the oh-so-perfect harmony of the world—this 'total work of art'—as outlined by Mondrian and De Stijl. Instead he absorbs the eternal, totalitarian order celebrated in abstract art into a vigorous figurative style, sensual and Apollonian, in which men in their new-found freedom resume their place in the simple cycle of life and work.   B.C.

Fernand Léger
Argentan 1881 - Gif-sur-Yvette 1955
The Country Outing, 1953
Oil on canvas; 130 x 161
Deposited by the National Museum
of Modern Art, 1986. Inv. D.86.1.1

Magnelli

'Art, if it is truly such, is not in the least abstract—everything is abstract and concrete at the same time.' This was the position taken up by Magnelli in the dispute between the adherents of figurative art and the supporters of the abstract. Though Magnelli, a Florentine by birth, fraternized with Parisian circles, knew the Italian Futurists, and took part, in 1944, in the first post-war Salon des Réalités Nouvelles, he took care, whilst always identifying with the aspirations of his age, never to pledge himself to any particular system. Magnelli's interest in painting began in 1907, at a time when 'In Florence ... isolated as we were ... one had to paint pictures that were completely made up'. In *The Countryside* (1914), reality is recognizable but is subordinated to certain rules: 'What counts more than anything is composition, the construction of the lay-out.' The colours are carefully worked out and applied in the 'precise quantity' required. In the euphoria following the 1918 victory, women bathing, women at their toilet are transformed into 'lyrical explosions', in a highly unusual artistic interlude during which form melts away. In 1920, in a development paralleling the 'return to order' then in full swing across Europe, Magnelli reintroduced the themes of peasants, houses, sailing boats—

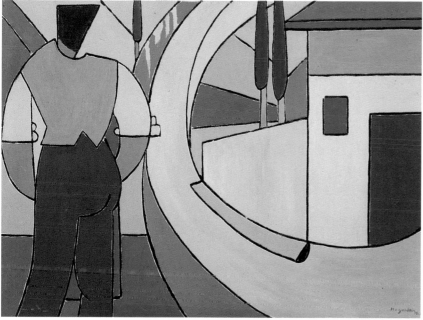

all treated in a highly realist manner. 1931 was a key date for the artist; it was in that year that his experience in the marble quarries at Carrara swung him towards a world of force and thrust, the world of the stone shattering under the chisel without preordained shape. *Stones/Painting GG* (1935) also reveals a taste for matter, in this case coarse jute canvas, making an undisguised appearance in the picture. Once in Paris, Magnelli gradually broke away from all figurative content, and in 1935-36 one begins to note the appearance of the highly characteristic forms observable in *Coloured Road* (1947) and which recur in Magnelli's work right up until 1971.

M.D.

Alberto Magnelli
Florence 1888 - Paris 1971
La campagna, 1913-14
Oil on canvas; 75.5 x 100
Purchased, 1973. Inv. 73.7.1

Alberto Magnelli
Florence 1888 - Paris 1971
Stones/Painting GG, 1935
Tempera on tarred jute canvas; 100 x 81
Given by Mme Susi Magnelli, 1980
Inv. 80.15.1

Marcel Duchamp
Blainville 1887 - Neuilly 1968
Boîte en Valise, 1936
Cardboard containing sixty-nine repro-
ductions or facsimiles; 39.8 x 35 x 8
Purchased, 1989. Inv. 89.6.1

Francis Picabia
Paris 1879 - Paris 1953
The Fiancé, 1916
Gouache and metallic paint on canvas;
26 x 33.5
Purchased, 1973. Inv. 73.8.3

Dada The outbreak of the First World War in 1914 put a brake on the forward-looking utopias that had characterized the artistic experimentation of the start of the century. The crisis in humanist values provoked by the war, and the rejection of a world that seemed destined to founder in a colossal bloodbath gave rise, in Zurich, amongst the members of an international circle of émigré intellectuals, to the anti-establishment movement popularized by its exponents under the extemporized, absurd, and provocative label of 'Dada'. Using a vocabulary still akin to Futurism, though rejecting the latter's bellicosity, Pierre Albert Birot's *War* (1914), with its ab-

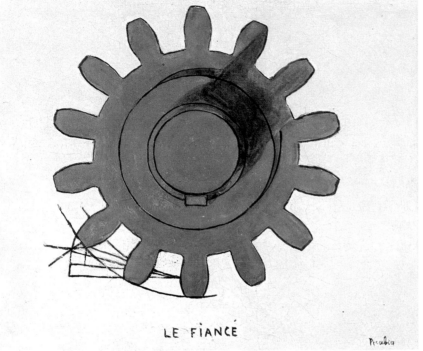

LE FIANCÉ

Picabia

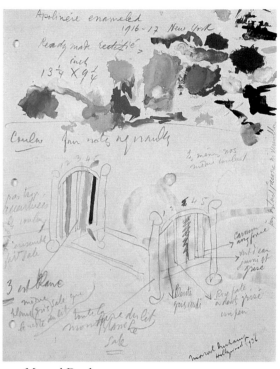

Marcel Duchamp
Blainville 1887 - Neuilly 1968
Apolinère Enameled
Gouache and pencil on paper, 1936
(contained in the *Boîte en Valise*)
Inv. 89.6.1

stract language based on rhythmical oppositions and clashes of colour, documents this feeling of tragedy and the sense of being wrenched apart experienced by many at that time. In *The Fiancé*, Picabia, more in line with the nihilist approach characteristic of Dada, displays an attitude of ironic detachment brimming with scepticism. The message conveyed by this picture is one of contempt for those values associated with mechanization and technical progress; the work projects an image of a humanity deprived of control over its actions, compelled to act outside its own will, like some paradoxical and enigmatic piece of machinery. In this respect, *The Fiancé* has much in common with the erotic machinery conceived by Duchamp in *The Bride Stripped Bare by Her Bachelors, Even*. Picabia's typical rejection of style and technique also has its parallel in the refusal to 'get drunk on turpentine' decreed by Duchamp. Indeed, from 1914, Duchamp abandoned painting, concentrating instead on making one or two 'artistic statements' (actions, creation of objects), and challenging the very processes of artistic activity. This approach was inaugurated with the renowned 'ready-mades', and was continued in the *Boîte en Valise*, begun in 1938. The idea of a personal, portable museum is a fine illustration of Duchamp's position: he believed that creativity was to be found more in

Overleaf:

Kurt Schwitters
Hanover 1887 - Ambleside (G.B.) 1948
Assemblage, c. 1939-44
Wood, pebbles, terracotta, glass, metal and paint on cardboard; 35 x 27
Purchased, 1974. Inv. 74.5.1

Raoul Hausmann
Vienna 1886 - Limoges 1971
Ventre de Carosse or Dupont-Durand Composes Poetry, 1920
Ink and watercolour on paper; 42.2 x 32
Purchased, 1976. Inv. 76.3.1

Pierre Albert-Birot
Angoulême 1876 - Paris 1966
War, 1916
Oil on canvas; 46 x 61
Deposited by the State. Inv. D.56.5.1

Anton Raederscheidt
Cologne 1892 - Cologne 1970
Three Figures, 1927
Charcoal on paper; 56.5 x 45.5
Purchased, 1974. Inv. 74.4.1

concepts than in the creation of specific aesthetic objects. This rejection of aesthetics is also common to the German Dadaist exponents of assemblage who considered that any object, any material, even the most base, could be called upon to play a part in a work of art. Distorting the sense of Cubist collages, Schwitters invented what we nowadays regard as 'the poetry of waste'. For this he used the countless objects discarded by an urban world all too ready to engage in wastefulness, or else, as in the late assemblage that figures in the Museum's collection, he recycled the debris—the poignant wreckage—that he had picked up on the sea-shore during his period of exile in Norway. Raoul Hausmann's watercolour *Ventre de Carosse* (Belly of a Coach, 1920) depicts to perfection the more biting and committed spirit of Dada, extending the metaphysical style of de Chirico in an attempt to demonstrate the absurdity of the condition imposed on man by modern society, and his total alienation. In Raederscheidt, who was active under the precarious Weimar order, the sense of the absurd is transformed into an oppressive vision—that of a partitioned and immured humanity, prefiguring in a more terrible form the isolation of Magritte's figuration (*Three Figures*, 1927). J.B.

Surrealism
Once stability had been restored, André Breton attempted, through Surrealism, to confer some positive meaning on Dadaist protest. Surrealism took as its authority the rebel poets of German Romanticism, or, in France, the works—then considered 'fringe'—of Rimbaud, Lautréamont, and Jarry, and it explored the new investigative methods made available by psychoanalysis. Its aim was to bring about a radical change in man and society, and to usher in a real revolution that would not only transform the material conditions of life, but fundamentally alter human thinking. With this in mind, the role assigned to art was to be primarily an experimental one. Art was to become a favoured means, for artists, of revealing unconscious phenomena and of throwing light on the true mechanisms of thought. Of all Surrealist painters, André Masson is undoubtedly the one who remained closest to the absolute automatism demanded by Breton in the 1924 manifesto. In *The Suitors* (1932), the rapidly executed elements come together to form a representational whole whose contents allude to a universal archetype, to fundamental human myths (in this case an episode from the *Odyssey*). This work is linked to the important series of depictions of massacres in which, in an explosion of violence and sexuality, the ambivalent (opposed and complementary) powers of Eros and Thanatos may be discerned. In *The Elk Hunt* (1932), the terse, cursive execution is transformed into ever more allusive representation, expressing the original predicament in a wild and instinctual manner. The picture was painted during the war, when Masson was in exile in the United States, and is one of the works that were to have a profound effect on the Action Painting generation of artists. The same primitive anguish emerges, in a different way, in *The Last Forest* (1960-70) by Max Ernst. The directed fortui-

André Masson
Balagny 1896 - Paris 1987
The Elk Hunt, 1942
Oil on canvas; 55 x 68.5
Purchased, 1982. Inv. 82.4.1

Yves Tanguy
Paris 1900 - Woodbury (US) 1955
Hands and Gloves, 1946
Oil on canvas; 92 x 71
Purchased, 1988. Inv. 88.13.1

André Masson
Balagny 1896 - Paris 1987
The Suitors, 1932
Oil on canvas; 78 x 168.7
Deposited by the National Museum
of Modern Art, 1984. Inv. D.84.6.5

Max Ernst
Brühl 1891 - Paris 1976
The Last Forest, 1960-70
Oil on canvas; 140 x 113
Deposited by the National Museum
of Modern Art, 1983. Inv. D.83.1.5

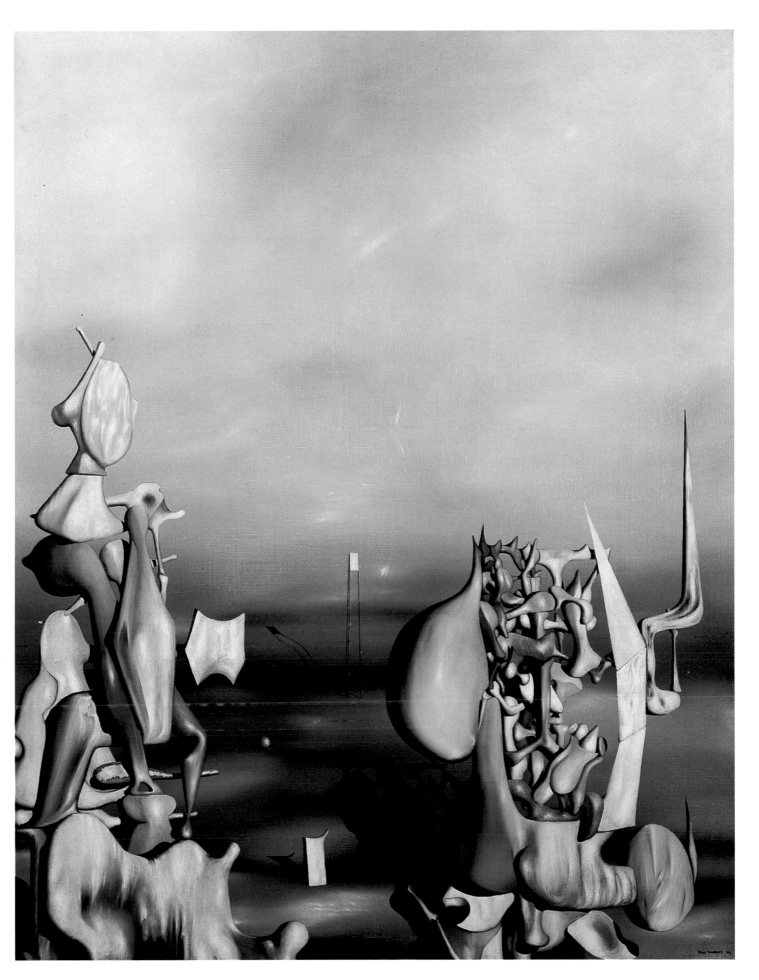

ties of grattage and frottage, taken up again from the 'forests' of the 1920s, produce a glaucous, tangled, proliferating, and shadowy world, the perfect setting for supernatural apparitions and a favoured scenario of early childhood fears. Miró's surrealism is also based on a constant invention of forms, but it is rarely 'black' in nature; instead it draws its inspiration—as shown by *Dancing Figures and Birds* (1968)—from spontaneity, humour, the refusal of heavyweight preoccupations, and a new-found ingenuity. Standing in contrast to such painters as these—for whom the exploration of unconscious phenomena necessarily brought with it the invention of new techniques—

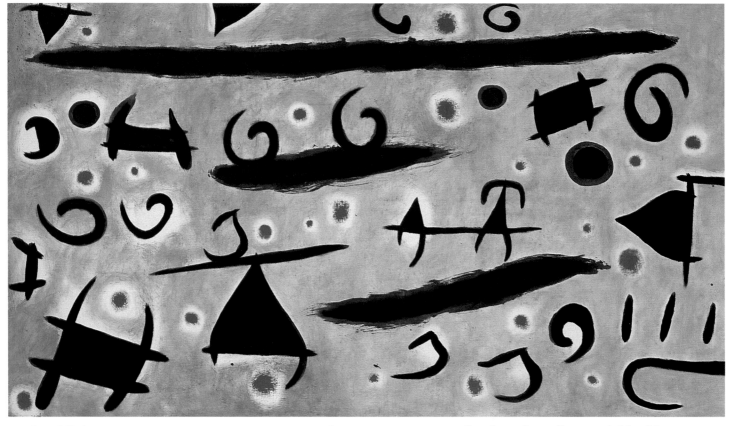

Joan Miró
Barcelona 1893 - Palma de Majorca 1983
Dancing Figures and Birds, 1968
Oil on canvas; 173 x 291
Deposed by the National Museum
of Modern Art, 1983. Inv. D.83.1.4

there was a category of artists whom Breton dubbed 'tracers of dreams'. Using a technique that aimed to produce the ultimate in *trompe-l'oeil* effect—described by Dali as 'simultaneous colour photography of images of concrete irrationality'—and basing themselves on the images furnished by the irrational, they attempted—as did, for example, the fanatically meticulous Tanguy (*Hands and Gloves*, 1946)—to capture the visions seen in dreams or in hallucinations, and express them in concrete form on the canvas. Tanguy's erratic landscapes, scattered with smooth, hard, biomorphic masses, give the impression of a fossilized world of forms eroded by wind and water and polished smooth by time. One feels the same disquieting uncertainty when confronted with the sculptures of Jean Arp: they have that same dual nature, hesitating between natural objects and dream-like creations—forms seen, just as the title says, *In Dreams* (1937). J.B.

Jean Arp
Strasbourg 1887 - Locarno 1966
In Dreams, 1937
Bronze ; 37 x 20 x 21
Given by the artist, 1957. Inv. 57.6.1

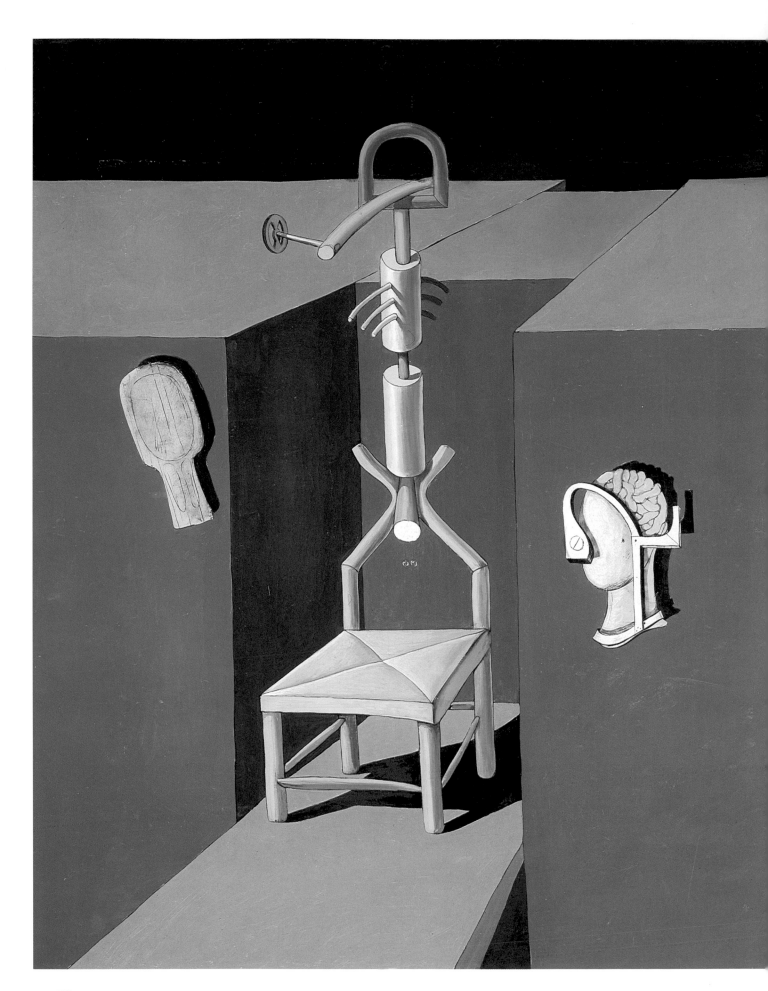

Victor Brauner

The most original feature of the Museum's Surrealist collection is undoubtedly the masterly series of works by Victor Brauner, bequeathed by Jacqueline Victor-Brauner. Works dating from the 1930s predominate, exhibiting an astounding variety of plastic techniques and an extraordinary wealth of creativity. One example is *Fantomas* (1932), where, in the labyrinth of a 'bachelor machine' closely resembling those created by Duchamp and Raymond Roussel, there appears the figure of the elusive hero of popular novels glorified by Breton and his group. Other examples are the paintings—such as *The Simulacrum* and *The Other Version* (1932)—in which incongruous assemblages, lacking any logical order yet dimly recalling the composite figure of a man, are set beneath the leaden sky of some metaphysical landscape.

In later years, Brauner's work was increasingly influenced by the esoteric, by the cabbala, witchcraft, and alchemy. Many of his paintings during this period contain religious symbolism and evoke initiation rites drawn both from ancient Egypt and from 'primitive' peoples (*The Philosophers' Stone*, 1940; *Sketch for Totintot*, 1942). During the war, Brauner was forced into hiding and found himself very short of materials, but, wishing

despite all this to continue his creative work, he began to use candle wax as a medium. Having created a number of small-scale works of rather rough and heavily laden appearance, he used the same procedure, after 1945, to produce pictures which, in contrast, display great refinement (*Oh Seasons*; *Oh Castles*, 1945). Brauner refused to be restricted to a particular style, and, at the start of the 1950s, he adopted a technique in which he displays a disconcerting combination of monochrome (grey camaïeu) and a nervous, incisive style of execution resembling that used earlier, within a realist framework, by Gruber and Giacometti (*Subjectivities*; *Co-existence*, 1952).

J.B.

Victor Brauner
Piatra Neamtz (Romania) 1903 -
Paris 1966
The Philosopher's Stone, 1940
Oil on canvas; 65.5 x 81.5
Jacqueline Victor-Brauner Bequest, 1987

Victor Brauner
Piatra Neamtz (Romania) 1903 -
Paris 1966
The Other Version, 1934
Oil on canvas; 92 x 73
Jacqueline Victor-Brauner Bequest, 1987

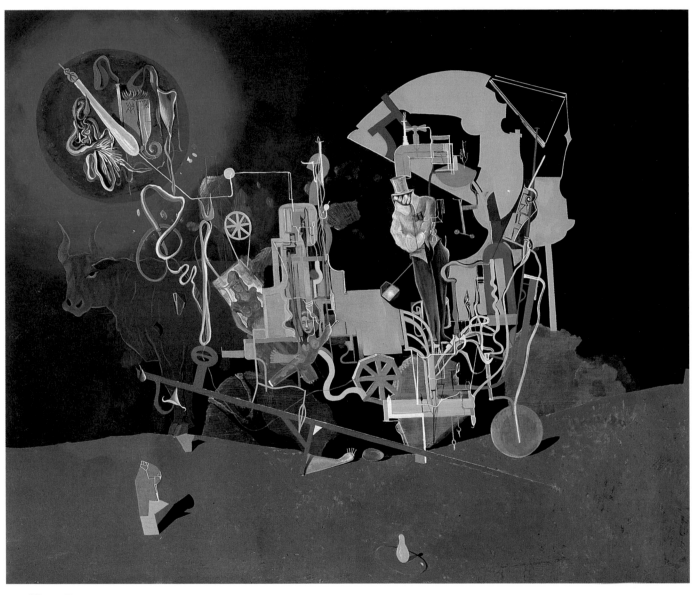

Victor Brauner
Piatra Neamtz (Romania) 1903 -
Paris 1966
Fantomas, 1932
Oil on canvas; 73 x 92
Jacqueline Victor-Brauner Bequest, 1987

Lionisiane, 1942
Pencil, Indian ink, watercolour on sheet
of herbarium; 32 x 20.5
Jacqueline Victor-Brauner Bequest, 1987

40

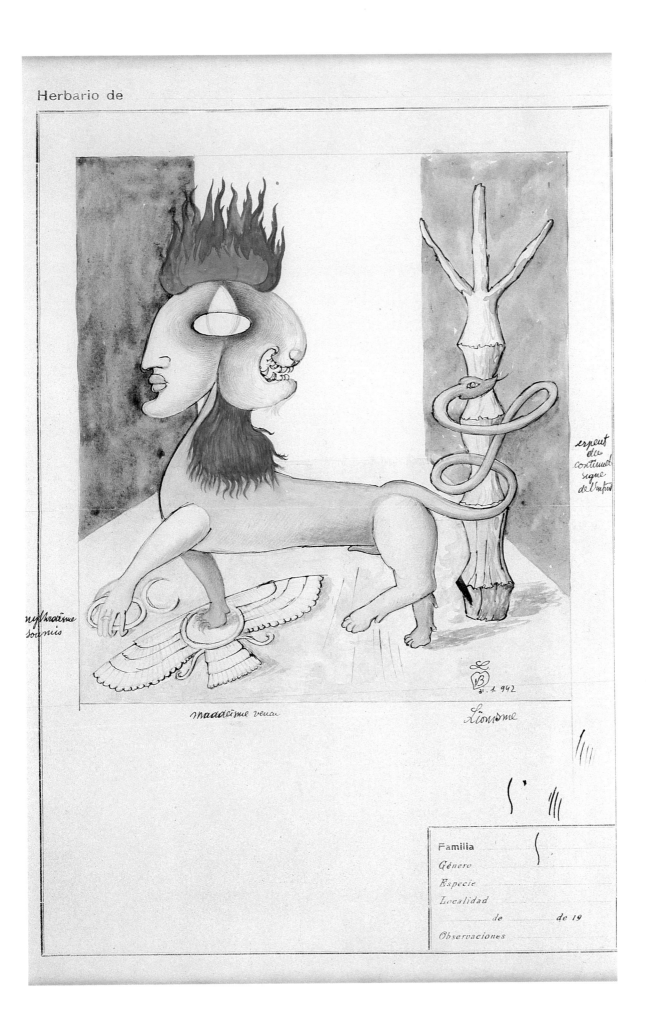

mythraïsme
soumis

maadeïsme venca

serpent
du
continuel
signe
de Vingal

Lïonisme

Familia

Género

Especie

Localidad

de ___ de 19

Observaciones

Raoul Dufy
Le Havre 1877 - Forcalquier 1953
Amphitrite, 1935-1953
Oil on canvas; 240 x 190
Deposited by the National Museum of
Modern Art, 1985. Inv. D.84.3.3

Art Deco

Apollinaire invented the term 'Orphism' to describe the work of Robert and Sonia Delaunay, two artists fascinated by the problem of colour. To convey the impression of light, they employed the principle of simultaneous contrast: colours interact yet retain complete autonomy. Robert Delaunay painted twenty-one portraits (1926-27) of the wife of the couturier Jacques Haim. And it was Sonia who designed the 'simultaneous' shawl worn by Mrs Heim. Sonia Delaunay shared the concerns of the creators of Art Deco in seeking to extend her experience and apply it to fashion and the decorative arts. She later returned to painting, displaying

Jean Dunand
Lancy (Switzerland) 1887 - 1942
Portrait of Mme Agnès, c. 1925
Tempera, collage, gold and silver leaf,
pencil on panel; 81.5 x 50
Given by A. and Y. Colcombet, 1950
Inv. 50.19.1

Gustave Miklos
Budapest 1888 - Oyonnax 1967
Head of a Woman, 1928
Patinated plaster; 56 x 25
Given by Mme Miklos, 1975. Inv. 75.7.5

a predilection—as in *Painting* (1960)—for disc-shapes.
Raoul Dufy also designed patterns for the superb textiles used by the couturiers Poiret and, later, Bianchini-Ferrier. In *Amphitrite* (1935-53), which was subsequently used as a design for an Aubusson tapestry, Dufy uses a highly supple graphic style, combining it with an ambient tone that influences each separate component of the composition. He also makes extremely poetic use of pictorial space. Dunand's *Mme Agnès*, executed on lacquer, depicts another famous couturière. During the 1930s, Dunand did the interior decoration for the

liner *Normandie*, furnishing it with sculpted panels of gilded lacquer. The Delaunays, Dunand, Miklos, and Marinot all took part in the 1925 International Exhibition of Decorative Arts, which featured the very latest products of Art Deco. Miklos created jewellery working with gold, silver, and gems, and this awoke in him an interest in sculpture. His huge hieratic sculptures, with their untrammelled lines and Cubist-inspired schematism, have often been labelled 'Byzantine Modernism'. Marinot, a painter and master glassmaker, produced some unprecedented effects of colour by introducing enamel or bubbles at the blowing stage. M.D.

Developments in Abstract Art
The move to forgo subject matter which occurred in France on the eve of the First World War gave rise to unparalleled artistic developments. Wether under the label of 'abstract' or of 'non-representational' art, the objective pursued by Kandinsky, Kupka, Mondrian, and others was to transcribe thoughts and intuitions on to canvas using the interplay of plane, line, form, and colour, and to proclaim the 'complete unfettered freedom of the artist to choose his means' (Kandinsky). A number of broad trends became apparent—for example, organic abstraction, as in Kupka's *Shape of Orange*, or geometric abstraction. For all those concerned, art was a quest for the ab-

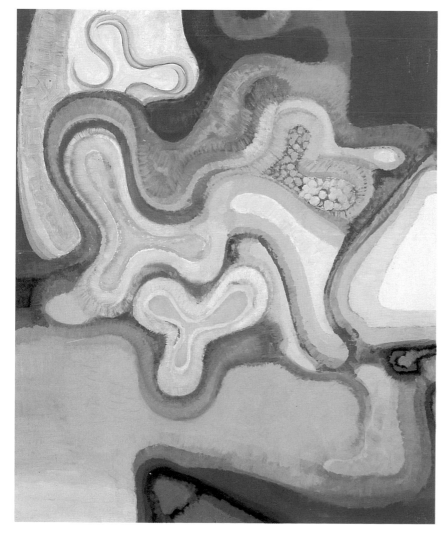

František Kupka
Opocno 1871 - Puteaux 1957
The Shape of Orange, 1923
Oil on canvas; 73 x 60
Deposited by the National Museum of Modern Art, 1966. Inv. D.66.4.2

Robert Delaunay
Paris 1885 - Montpellier 1941
Portrait of Mrs Heim, 1926-27
Oil on canvas; 130 x 97
Deposited by the National Museum of Modern Art, 1984. Inv. D.84.3.1

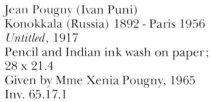

Jean Pougny (Ivan Puni)
Konokkala (Russia) 1892 - Paris 1956
Untitled, 1917
Pencil and Indian ink wash on paper;
28 x 21.4
Given by Mme Xenia Pougny, 1965
Inv. 65.17.1

Lajos Kassak
Ersekujvar (Hungary) 1887 -
Budapest 1967
Popular Motifs, 1921
Gouache on paper; 26.3 x 19.8
Deposited by the State, 1966
Inv. D.66.2.1

Marcelle Cahn
Strasbourg 1895 - Neuilly 1981
Plane, Aviatic Form, 1930
Oil on canvas; 60 x 73.5
Given by the artist, 1957. Inv. 57.3.1

Wassily Kandinsky
Moscow 1866 - Neuilly-sur-Seine 1944
Composition IX, 1936
Oil on canvas; 113.5 x 195
Deposited by the National Museum
of Modern Art, 1986. Inv. D.86.1.4

Overleaf:

Otto Freundlich
Stolp (Pomerania) 1878 -
Lublin (Poland) 1943
Composition, 1930
Oil on canvas; 116 x 89
Purchased, 1957. Inv. 57.7.1

César Domela (Amsterdam 1900)
Neo-Plastic Composition No. 5-1, 1926
Oil on canvas; 83 x 51
Purchased, 1989. Inv. 89.24.1

48

Louis Fernandez
Oviedo (Asturias) 1900 - Paris 1963
Mock-up of Grey Abstraction No. 51, 1933
Oil on canvas; 36.5 x 24.5
Purchased, 1972. Inv. 72.7.1

solute, vindicated in various—often divergent—writings. During the 1920s, Otto Freundlich created his own plastic technique. In *Composition* (1930), a series of little forms of proximate tonality are juxtaposed, arranged around a basic schema of curves. Freundlich uses his 'proto-elements of new objective painting' to fragment the two-dimensional plane of the canvas and create an energy motivated by colour. Freundlich set his work within a framework of spiritual and political reflection. Being a Jew, a German, and an abstract artist, he was a prime target for the Nazis.

Mondrian, Van Doesburg, and the journal *De Stijl* all exerted an influence on artists such as Domela and Gorin. Mondrian, with his Neo-Plasticism, had issued strict rules based on the use of straight lines intersecting at right angles and on the use of the three colours red, yellow, and blue. The function of the straight line was to purge all feeling from the painting. César Domela occupies a position between Mondrian and Van Doesburg. In *Neo-Plastic Composition No. 5-1* (1926), the straight lines are inclined as decreed in the *Manifesto of Elementarism* (Van Doesburg's proclamation of the rule of the inclined plane). Domela was involved in the frenetic cultural activity that was taking place across Europe at this time: publication of articles in journals, founding of movements such as Cercle et Carré and Abstraction-Création. These latter were associations of artists, in some cases holding different points of view but all feeling the need to come together to demonstrate their adherence to new forms of expression. In a work of 1917—perhaps a sketch for a Constructivist relief—Ivan Puni uses an Indian-ink wash to create a series of forms unrelated to any subject and clearly recalling Malevich and Tatlin, still the two pre-eminent artistic forces of the day.

Kandinsky fled to France—to Paris—in 1933. Ever faithful to his spiritualist aspirations, he took an interest in the tiniest, most secret forms of life, as depicted in the catalogues published by pharmaceutical companies. In *Composition IX* (1936), a whole world of organic forms is suspended in an interplay of undulating curves. Confronted with abstract art, a number of individuals such as Le Corbusier and Ozenfant raised their voices in protest. Although taking Cubism as their starting-point and admitting the untrammelled lines of geometric abstraction, they spoke out, through the Purist movement, founded in 1918, in defence of art based on reality. Marcelle Cahn was an adherent of this doctrine. In *The Roofs* of 1927, and in *Aviatic Form* (1930), she creates a dematerialized world in which every element corresponds to a superior, universal order. M.D.

Jean Hélion The Museum has five paintings by Jean Hélion, of which four were acquired thanks to the generosity of the artist himself, of Jacqueline Victor-Brauner, and of a private collector. Three are key works marking turning-points in Hélion's art. The small painting *Equilibrium* of 1933, for example, marks the abandonment by the artist of the principles of composition developed by the De Stijl group and which he had applied since he had helped found the Art Concret circle

Jean Hélion
Couterne 1904 - Paris 1987
Equilibrium, 1933
Oil on canvas; 54 x 64.5
Given by the artist, 1978. Inv. 78.7.2

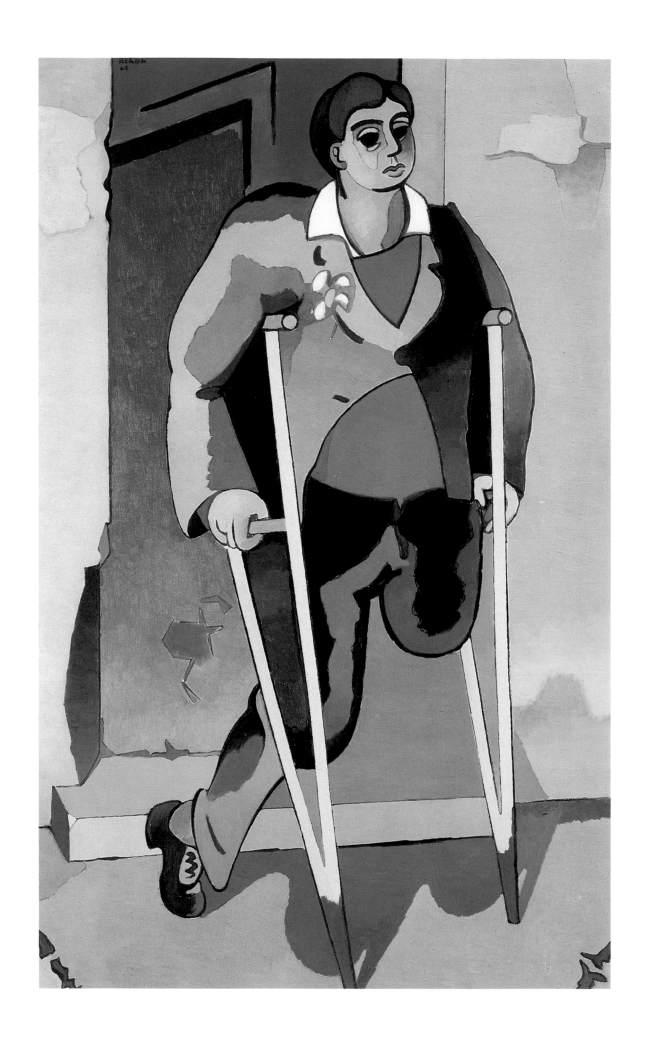

with Van Doesburg, Tutundjian, and Carlsund in 1929. The influence of Léger is visible in the firmly modelled volumes, which are neither totally organic nor totally geometric, although they might have been stamped out by machine. Soon after this, Hélion's *Figures*—a 'humanist' synthesis of Léger's art and the 'Purism' of Le Corbusier and Ozenfant—made their appearance. These are abstract manifestations of the anxiety and confusion felt by Hélion at this time. Faced with an increasingly dangerous situation, he decided to abandon the hermetism of abstract art, which, he considered, was incapable of responding to the demands of history.

Having escaped, in 1942, from a prison camp in Pomerania, he returned to the United States, where he had been a frequent visitor since 1932. Here he set out on a realist path, the ultimate goal of which—well illustrated in *Gothic Figure* and *Scène journalière*—was to express reality using the means which twentieth-century art had developed for constructing a tangible order on the basis of 'pure' plastic signs. During the 1950s, Hélion worked against the prevailing trend and engaged in a meticulous rendering of reality reminiscent of Gruber's obsessive 'verism'. *Victor's Walk*, an unfinished work, is like a 'Joycian' fragment depicting one particular moment in life, a pictorial anticipation of the 'nouveau roman'. This *non finito* demonstrates the impossibility, in terms of the concrete reality of a painting, of achieving an exact reproduction of reality, and, following this, the artist sought to restore the substance of that reality through the use of simple signs combining plane, shape, and colour.   B.C.

Jean Hélion
Couterne 1904 - Paris 1987
Scène journalière, 1948
Oil on canvas; 50 x 65.2
Jacqueline Victor-Brauner Bequest, 1987

Jean Hélion
Couterne 1904 - Paris 1987
Gothic Figure, 1945
Oil on canvas; 116.5 x 73
Purchased, 1978. Inv. 78.7.1

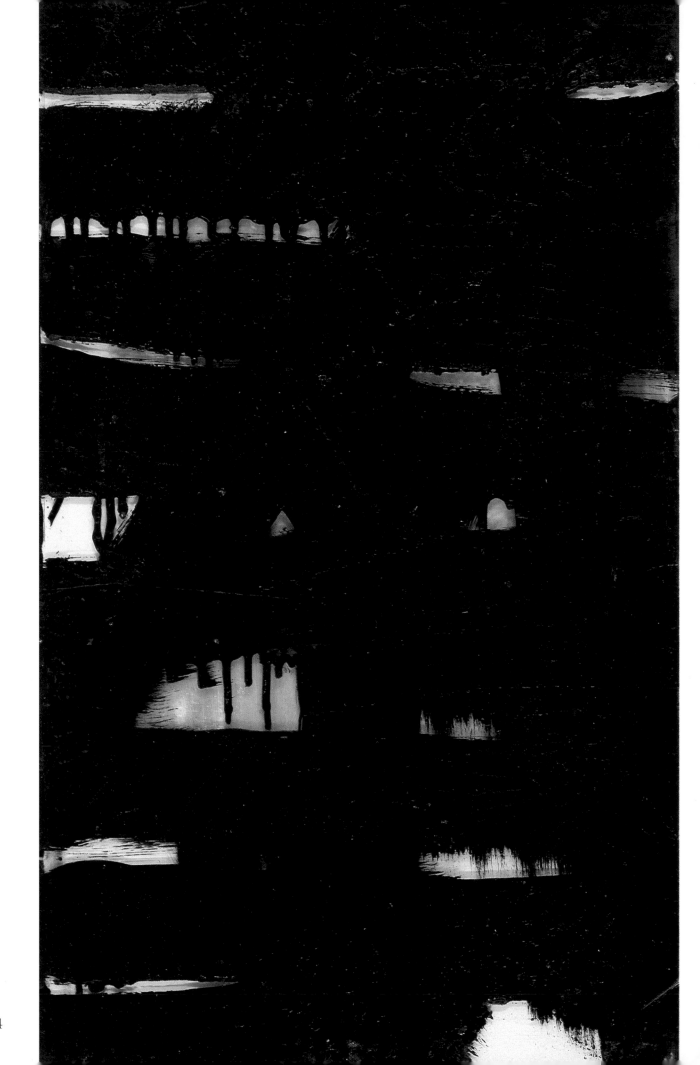

The 1950s

The collection held by the Saint-Etienne Museum of Modern Art of works by artists who came to prominence in the post-war period is, without a doubt, one of the most important of its kind in France, despite its lack of works by the New York School. These had already become unattainable when the Museum eventually found itself in a position to acquire paintings and sculptures by major artists who had worked, or were still working in Paris, and in France in general. In many respects, this collection remains deficient. Yet it provides a good illustration of the history of French museums and of their relationship to contemporary art—a fact which leads one to reassess a number of received ideas. The imperialism of the Ecole the Paris, and its still oft-criticized omnipresence, cannot really be said to have made themselves felt in French collections. The history of this so-called school will not be able to be written exclusively on the basis of the works preserved in French museums. As far as the Museum of Saint-Etienne is concerned, it was only in the last few years that major works by Bissière, Manessier, Atlan, Poliakoff, and others could be brought together and displayed. The works of Bissière and Manessier exhibited in the Museum are remarkable illustrations of the quest of those painters who sought, during those dark days, to defend and exemplify their own conception of French tradition, attempting to extend it along the path of modernity, as against those who sought to divert it into a reactionary 'full speed astern'. These artists were non-figurative in the sense that they rejected a representation of reality in which the latter was reduced to an anecdotal account based on fluctuating appearance; they attempted—like the American painters of their generation, though in a different historical context—to embody, in basic intrinsic signs on canvas, the profound truth of a landscape, its light, and that element which links it to the experience of those who inhabit it. If one excepts Socialist Realism, not represented in the collection, and geometric abstraction, amply illustrated in works—by Vasarely, Gorin, and Herbin—expressing forward-looking convictions and the inexorable advent of a Superior Order, the post-war years are characterized above all by an affirmation of the individual in his relationship to a world and a reality that no longer correspond to the humanist creed. The frailty of that creed had been made manifest by the war, the concentration camps, and the Bomb. Morellet's geometry, as opposed to Vasarely's or Schöffer's, belongs to the domain of the arbitrary, the random, the insignificant. This gratuitous-

Pierre Soulages (Rodez 1919)
Untitled, 1948
Tar on glass; 76.5 x 45.5
Given by the artist, 1985. Inv. 85.82.1

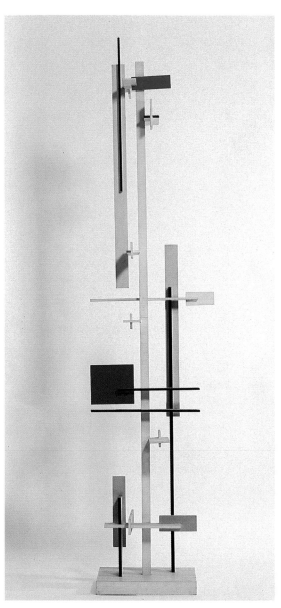

Jean Gorin
Saint-Emilien-de-Blain 1899 - Niort 1981
Spatio-Temporal Plastic Construction No. 9,
1955
Oil-painted wood; 250 x 50.5 x 50.5
Given by the artist, 1969. Inv. 69.3.1

ness sets up a kind of 'logic' and 'casualty' reminiscent of Duchamp's absurd rationalism. In the work by Morellet held at Saint-Etienne one can also discern a kind of 'premonition' of Conceptual and Minimal Art. This all goes to show that the definitive history of art in France during the 1950s is far from written. One cannot, for example, continue to classify the works of Hartung and Soulages under the heading of gestural abstraction, when it appears increasingly difficult to identify in them its characteristic forms and the particular meaning it would confer on them. The goal of Hartung's art is the perfection of methods of achieving his own objectives. The lines, serpentine windings, and elongations of paint which allow one to 'relive' the rapid movements of execution are far from being mere effects of chance or automatism. They crystallize an aesthetic and an ethic geared to achieving the highest perfection. This same quest for the absolute is present in the timeless works of Pierre Soulages, of which the Museum owns a rare collection. In these, painting is reduced to exemplary simplicity, as illustrated by the three tar-on-glass paintings—executed well before the appearance of Franz Kline's peremptory signs. Light is the real subject of this painting, a light born of the pigment, the colour, and the artist's labour—slow, well thought out, and conscious, but never systematic. The same is true of Fautrier's work. And of Dubuffet's, of which the Museum has managed, through deposits from the National Museum of Modern Art, to assemble eleven examples, including a *Texturology* that highlights the divide separating Dubuffet in the 1950s from the abstract landscape-art then in vogue. The concentration on different types of soil, which Dubuffet seeks to 'reconstitute' by a patient and humble process of kneading of the paint, reduces the painting to a coarse yet splendid materiality. The artist's 'last' works, such as those of the 'Hourloupe' period, similarly defy classification and historical order. In these, Dubuffet's choice of forms, his puzzle-like agglutinations of 'modules', enable him to construct a world—his own world—reminiscent of those constructed, as an escape from the real world, by the 'acculturated' creators brought together by the artist in his museum of Art Brut. Dubuffet's primitivism is that of the common man, rebelling against all convention, and is quite unclassifiable.

His works are in harmony with those of the new generation of the early 1980s, which rejected the inexorable advance of an illusorily progressive modernity. If one adds to these collections a harrowing work by Fautrier, with its scraped paint and acid colours; the intense, incisively drawn figures of Victor Brauner; Germaine Richier's anthropomorphized mantis; a huge work by Simon Hantaï, in which the paint is made to peel away in the reiteration of an obsessive gesture; and finally two magnificent paintings of glacial starkness by Bram Van Velde—one may see how the Museum of Modern Art's collection bears witness to what might at that time have been termed the Sisyphean efforts made by artists after the war to restore meaning to the acts of painting and sculpting.   B.C.

56

Geometric Abstraction

Abstract geometric art of the period following the Second World War is represented in the Museum's collection by a well-knit group of works, reinforced by a number of recent, opportune acquisitions. Indeed, with the acquisition of Josef Albers' *Homage to the Square (Silent Abode)*, the collection is more than merely enriched: it has diversified by incorporating the work of a major American artist, and it now reveals how geometric abstractionists, despite their choice of a single corpus of forms, engaged in complex and varied research.

From the time that he and his brother, Naum Gabo, issued the Realistic Manifesto in 1919, Antoine Pevsner's conception of sculpture remained essentially unchanged. The alterations

Josef Albers
Bottrop (Westphalia) 1988 -
Orange (Connectitut) 1976
Homage to the Square (Silent Abode), 1954
Oil on masonite; 80.7 x 80.7
Purchased, 1989. Inv. 89.15.1

he did make to his work related more to diversification of materials (plaster, bronze, plastic, cement, etc.) than to any real change in his approach to the construction of volumes, to the modulation of forms, which he grooved with metal thread, or to the interplay of solids and voids, where shadow nestles and light reaches outwards. Thus the *Extendible Victory Column* remains faithful to the remarkable and powerful expansion of form that is so typical of the artist's work.

With Jean Gorin's *Spatio-Temporal Plastic Construction No. 9*, the tenets of Neo-Plasticism, as defined by Piet Mondrian at the beginning of the century, are reasserted with rigour and

Robert Jacobsen (Copenhagen, 1912)
Invisible Victory, 1957
Welded iron; 62.1 x 46 x 22.1
Deposited by the State, 1967
Inv. D.67.1.2

Auguste Herbin
Quievy 1882 - Paris 1960
Thursday, 1950
Oil on canvas; 55 x 46
Purchased, 1981. Inv. 81.9.1

discipline. There is a reaffirmation of that harmonious vision of a world from which all trace of individual expressionism has been banished. In Victor Vasarely's *Hargita* we see the beginnings of research that was soon to posit a type of art based on the interaction of colour and movement. This research—in no way to be dismissed as mere decoration—marked a real commitment to the construction of the city of the future, an ideal of functionality, formal beauty, and transparency of operation.

The Danish sculptor Robert Jacobson welds together metal components, thus sculpting space itself, with solids and voids forming interdependent, perfectly allied components.

In his *Mobile 6.5.1.4*, Alexander Calder, more than ten years older than the last two artists mentioned, pursues research

Victor Vasarely (Pecs, Hungary, 1908)
Hargita (or *Barlovanto*), 1950-53
Oil on hardboard; 86.2 x 79.8
Given by the artist, 1959. Inv. 59.12.1

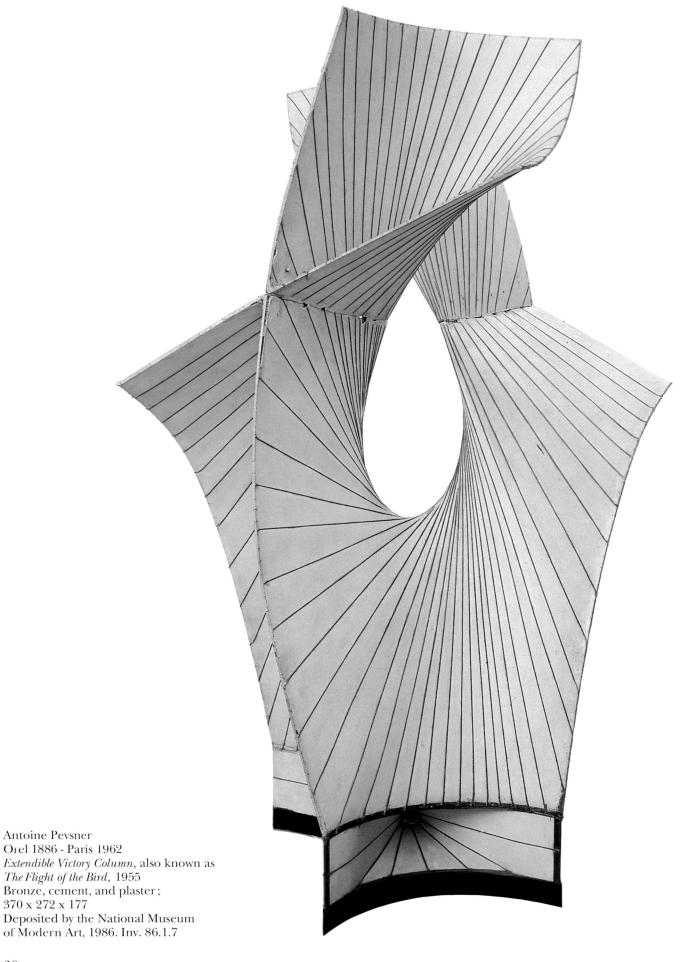

Antoine Pevsner
Orel 1886 - Paris 1962
Extendible Victory Column, also known as
The Flight of the Bird, 1955
Bronze, cement, and plaster;
370 x 272 x 177
Deposited by the National Museum
of Modern Art, 1986. Inv. 86.1.7

60

begun during the 1930s, in which painted metal shapes, activated simply by air currents, form what may be termed 'painting in space'. This attempt to break down the barriers between traditional artistic disciplines was a radical lesson to the younger generation, opening up a new path which they subsequently opted to follow. *Three Wings* of 1963 forms part of the 'stabile' series. In it, monumental shapes are traced out in space, their powerful rhythms maintaining a remarkable dynamism.

Etienne Beothy, who, like Alexander Calder, had a scientific training, displays a faultless technical mastery enabling him to project into space smooth, sinuous abstract shapes that are as near to perfection as possible. Thus the sculptor attempts to give concrete expression to forms that belong more to the usual repertoire of lyrical art.

Through his attempts to develop a coherent vocabulary that would take account not only of colour and form but also of letter and sound, Auguste Herbin sought to revive the age-old dream of a style of art still open to symbolism and endowed with a certain spiritual profundity. *Thursday* (1950) is a fine example of painting conceived of as a system of visual signs, a veritable 'foundation course' for social change.

After the war, and following the activities of the Cercle et Carré and Abstraction-Création movements, to which many of the artists in this collection had belonged in the 1930s, geometric abstraction won historical recognition. Sonia Delaunay and Alberto Magnelli contributed to this process through their unceasing investigative work. Yet their artistic activity was not confined to the first half of the century, as witnessed by the works preserved in Saint-Etienne. The 1960 *Painting*, together with almost sixty lithographs, allow one to appreciate just how intense was Sonia Delaunay's activity. The same applies to Magnelli (see the relevant section on him). *Homage to the Square* by Josef Albers is one of a long series of

François Morellet (Cholet 1926)
3,200 Squares
Oil on canvas; 160 x 320
Purchased, 1987. Inv. 87.10.1

61

works on this theme, begun at the close of the 1940s. This American artist, displaying an admirably methodical turn of mind, embarked on a contemplation—bordering on meditation—of the interaction of colours concentrated in a stable form. In so doing he inaugurated research that was to be taken up by kinetic artists working around 1960. François Morellet also offers a kind of tribute to the square when he reproduces it 3,200 times on his canvas. Displaying a certain degree of irony, Morellet's procedure leaves room for chance and risk, at the same time preserving rigour and method.

To complete this brief survey of post-war geometric abstrac-

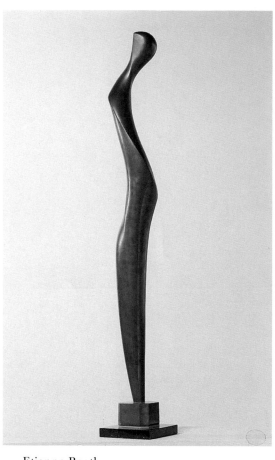

Etienne Beothy
Heves (Hungary) 1897 - Paris 1961
Complaint, 1958
Polished bronze; 130
Given by the artist, 1959. Inv. 59.5.1

Alexander Calder
Philadelphia 1898 - New York 1976
Mobile 6.5.1.4, c. 1950
Painted metal; approx. 150
Purchased, 1955. Inv. 55.9.1

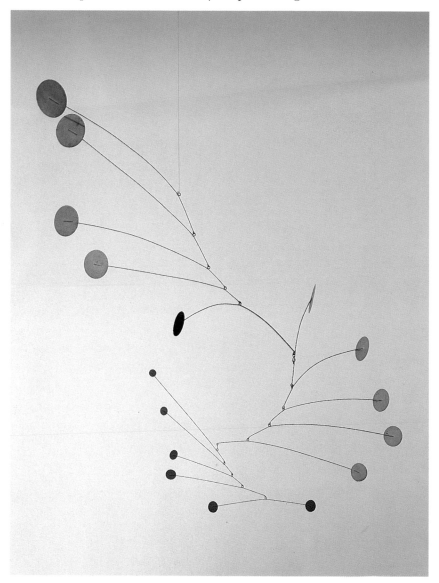

tion, we should indicate the presence in the Museum's collection of works by the Uruguayan artist Arden Quin, the founder of the Madi movement, and by the French artists Leppien and Lempereur-Haut.   M.F.

Sonia Delaunay
Odessa 1885 - Paris 1979
Painting, 1960
Oil on canvas; 130 x 162
Deposited by the National Museum
of Modern Art, 1984. Inv. D.84.3.2

The Post-War Generation

In 1940-45 the activity of avant-garde artists was halted. Under threat from the Nazi regime, these artists went into exile or sought safety in a semi-clandestine life-style—though traces of artistic activity, and even of opposition to the rules imposed by authorities, did persist. But Bazaine, Lapicque, Le Moal, Manessier, Estève, and others would have to wait for hostilities to be over before expressing themselves openly. In 1945 Paris seemed to assert its pre-eminence as the arts capital of the world, retaining this status until the 1960s. Roger Bissière, already an established artist before the war, became interested in means of

Alfred Manessier (Saint-Ouen, 1911)
Morning Space, 1949
Oil on canvas; 131 x 162
Deposited by the National Museum
of Modern Art, 1983. Inv. D.83.1.2

expression which had become neglected at that time. He executed a number of frescos, notably for the great exhibition of 1937. In 1939, having withdrawn to Boissiérette, his main concern was to revitalize himself by drawing on sources that had been obscured or forgotten: folk art, Romanesque art, the art of Grünewald and Hieronymus Bosch. In *Ochre and Blue* (1953), grids of rough black lines criss-cross the canvas, the spaces between enclosing dabs of colour. This work marks a return to a simple style of art that goes straight to essentials and links back to a certain religious tradition. Accord-

Serge Poliakoff
Moscow 1900 - Paris 1969
Composition, 1956
Oil on canvas; 130 x 97
Deposited by the National Museum
of Modern Art, 1983. Inv. D.83.1.3

Jean Atlan
Constantine 1913 - Villiers 1960
Amaryllis, 1959
Oil on canvas; 130 x 81
Deposited by the National Museum of
Modern Art, 1983. Inv. D.83.1.1

Roger Bissière
Villeréal 1888 - Boissiérette 1964
Ochre and Blue, 1953
Egg tempera on canvas; 49 x 91
Purchased, 1981. Inv. 81.8.1

ing to Alfred Manessier, a former pupil—like Le Moal—of Bissière's, *Morning Space* (1949) uses a language that appears abstract but has a non-abstract content. The aim is for the artist to express a certain quality of internal emotion, to 'go back to his reality and become aware once again of that which is essential in him'.

The grid of long grey lines is reminiscent, as is Le Moal's *Village on the Bay* (1951), of the 'Cubist grid', and represents a type of Cubism which art historians of the 1940s regarded as fitting into a particular French tradition. Bissière, a man of profound religious conviction and a deep lover of nature,

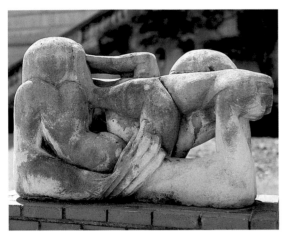

Etienne Martin (Loriol 1913)
Couple, 1956 (retouched 1962)
Limestone; 90 x 142 x 61
Purchased, 1961. Inv. 61.10.1

Jean Le Moal (Authon-du-Perche 1909)
Village on the Bay, 1951
Oil on canvas; 38.4 x 61.5
Purchased, 1951. Inv. 51.15.1

also drew inspiration from the art of the stained-glass window. Jean-Michel Atlan, educated on a diet of poetry and philosophy, turned to a different set of traditions for inspiration. He began, in 1944, by writing poetry but went on to become a self-taught painter. He kept his mind constantly open to the 'fundamental forces of nature', and he realized the tenuousness of the barrier that separates the normal from the peculiar. In *Amaryllis* (1959), dominated by the rhythms of the world of vegetation, Atlan used a broad black outline, varying its intensity and creating a thick, rich material that contributes to the mystery of the work.

Serge Poliakoff's art is also the product of contact with works from the past—icons, Ravenna mosaics, frescos by Giotto. He creates his forms stroke by stroke, applying broad flat areas of non-uniform colour that gradually assume a shape and are subordinated one to the other. Poliakoff is an artist in search of the absolute, seemingly belonging more to a lyrical than to a purely geometric trend.

Francis Gruber, resolutely realist, creates an impression of strangeness by laying stress on reality itself. Like his contemporaries, he was an admirer of the Primitives. As an artist, he was isolated, suffering from ill-health. He worked in his studio, casting a keen eye on all that surrounded him. The attitudes struck by the human figures he depicts are compelling rather than elegant: the melancholy posture of Mia in *Seated Woman Mia* (1933) rouses the curiosity; it is a disquieting feature in a setting that is otherwise banal, except for the still life in the foreground, with its Cubist allusions. Are

Gruber's scenarios perhaps intended as warnings? Do they perhaps herald the great existential questions that sprang from the torments of the war and the Holocaust?   M.D.

Francis Gruber
Nancy 1912 - Paris 1948
Young Woman in an Interior, Mia, 1933
Oil on canvas; 204 x 204.6
Purchased, 1988. Inv. 89.14.1

Bram Van Velde
Zoeterwoude (Netherlands) 1895 -
Grimaud, 1981
Painting, 1956
Oil on canvas; 170 x 243
Purchased, 1984. Inv. 84.5.1

Gestural Painting

In about 1950, a type of painting emerged which contrasted with the affirmative style of previous trends and inaugurated a lengthy period of questioning of experience. Its distinguishing features were gesture, mark, and the impress of gesture itself, diverse in its forms and in that which underlies it. Hence what has been labelled 'gestural painting' for ease of classification in fact conceals as many techniques as there are artists. The Museum's collection of works from this period is certainly not exhaustive, but it does give a good account of the main issues of the day. Covering as it does artists ranging from Hans Hartung to

Camille Bryen
Nantes 1907 - Paris 1977
Crinane Jaune, 1953
Oil on canvas; 101 x 74
Purchased, 1982. Inv. 82.1.1

Hans Hartung
Leipzig 1904 - Antibes 1990
T.1949-1, 1949
Oil on hardboard; 93 x 136
Purchased, 1982. Inv. 82.13.1

Olivier Debré, from Camille Bryen to Bram Van Velde, the collection affords ample material to enable one to identify the questions raised in this crucial period—even though in most cases we know these to be without an answer.

Two years after his first one-man exhibition at Lydia Conti's, and one year after the memorable HWPSMTB exhibition at the Colette Allendy Gallery in Paris, Hans Hartung completed the work entitled *T.1949-1*, now part of the Museum's collection. Executed on hardboard, as if to push the work to greater brilliance, this picture forms part of a process of research that began in the 1920s and was resumed some years later. The aim is not to paint the support but to act on it, in order to record on it, in the surest way possible, the passage of time, which, for Hartung, involves active contemplation of cosmic space. Gaping space and the recording of duration—these are the bases of the gestural style practised by Hartung, and the painting housed in the Museum, with its firm lines and powerful colours, is no doubt one of the most radical statements of that style.

The situation is quite different with Bram Van Velde in whose work gesture is an expression of all the uncertainties experienced in the face of existence. The earliest work housed in the Museum dates from about 1932, a period of great hardship for Van Velde, when lack of money forced him into exile in Majorca, because life there was cheaper. The human figures, landscapes and still lifes that had occupied the artist's canvases up to that point gradually dissolved into a tangle of dislocated forms. A larger-format work of 1956 entitled *Painting* no longer allows of any reference to external reality. Like the man himself, the painting has begun a depressing process of collapse: fragmented shapes and furrowed colours are all that break the silence of a man who knows that no words, no doctrine is to be trusted, and that only experience can provide a way forward.

Bram Van Velde was not the only one to experience this kind of mistrust of language. This is surely also what prompts Camille Bryen—the author of a piece of *Unwriting*—to his un-

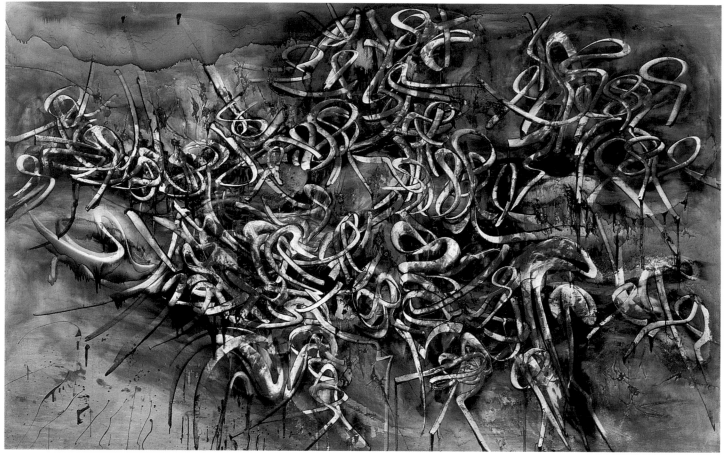

Simon Hantaï (Bia, Hungary, 1922)
Painting, 1955
Oil on canvas; 175 x 277
Purchased, 1980. Inv. 80.8.1

usual and ironic manipulation of it. Bryen, artist-cum-poet, plays havoc with spelling and grammar and takes delight in inventing new words. *Crinane Jaune*, the title of the Bryen canvas acquired by the Museum, is a phrase taken from the phonetic poem, *Hépérile* written in 1950. The language-painting link is based on this same negation of rule and expression. Hence the 'formless' *(informel)* character of the whole work: words are destroyed, meaning is exhausted, form dissolves. In pieces such as this Camille Bryen is moving on from the works of the 1930s, in which the Dadaist inspiration is clearly visible, to the statement of a primitive human condition in which man, untainted by culture, retains his powers of creativity intact.

Simon Hantaï's *Painting* (1955) reveals a further aspect of gestural abstract art. Hantaï, a Hungarian artist who emigrated to France in 1949, quickly established links with the Surrealists. In this picture he uses a technique developed by

Olivier Debré (Paris 1920)
Ochre, Purple Stain, 1970
Oil on canvas; 195 x 190
Purchased, 1974. Inv. 74.7.1

Masson, Ernst, and Miró, in which the automatic nature of gesture is given pride of place. The format selected by the artist lends itself well to the syncopated dance in which the artist's body, interacting in an almost erotic way with the canvas, becomes totally absorbed. The result is a work that displays a multiplicity of graphic forms; coatings, dribblings, scratchings, scrapings. Hantaï seems here to want to exorcise gesture, later gradually eliminating it, and eventually coming round to an increasingly methodical style of art.

Ochre, Purple Stain is unquestionably one of Olivier Debré's *chefs-d'oeuvre*. The painting was executed when the artist had attained a high degree of maturity; the resulting gesture and line constitute what might be regarded as a memory of time past. Such gestural work, though important, does not itself adequately define Debré's painting. To appreciate its range, one needs to recall Debré's reflections on nature, and, more particularly, his careful observation of light in the countryside around the Loire.

The Museum's collections, which also comprise works by Messagier, Hosiasson, Crippa, and others, reveal the differences in approach of those artists who, for the sake of ease, have historically been grouped together under the generic term of gestural painting.   M.F.

Pierre Soulages
Pierre Soulages is represented in the Museum's collection by an extremely important set of works. Three 1947 tar-on-glass compositions, a 1959 oil, and another oil, dated 1979, provide enough material to familiarize us, if not with the development of Soulages' work—so resistant to any chronological treatment—at least with the

different procedures used by the artist since the post-war period to achieve his objectives. These objectives remain unchanged today. Soulages believes that painting must be the crucible in which light is produced, and—seemingly paradoxically, yet not so—his chosen method has been to give increasing prominence to the colour black. The Museum's tar-on-glass compositions belong to his early style. Material and support are confronted, and this encounter, at once antagonistic and complementary, combining opacity and transparency, produces the desired impression of light. In the 1959 painting, light crosses a pictorial space cluttered with broad, sombre-toned marks, managing still to distinguish itself from the paint spread across the canvas with tools fashioned by the artist's own hand. In the 1979 work, the light emanates from the paint itself, which covers practically the whole canvas. The light now oozes—rather than springs—from the black itself, thus acquiring highly subtle nuances.

M.F.

Dubuffet

Following the outcry provoked by his first exhibition, at the Drouin Gallery in 1944, Jean Dubuffet never ceased to advertise, both in his painting and in his numerous

Pierre Soulages (Rodez 1919)
Painting, 18 April 1959
Oil on canvas; 130 x 162
Purchased, 1985. Inv. 85.81.1

Jean Dubuffet
Le Havre 1901 - Paris 1985
Texturology XLVII (Innate Life), 1958
Oil on canvas; 89 x 130
Purchased, 1974. Inv. 74.3.1

writings, his contempt for culture and for art as propagated by museums and those who teach it. His work was aimed at denouncing what he saw as the ossifying, inhibiting, and suffocating nature of cultural practices that preclude any truly original and genuine expression by the individual. Against the paradigmatic power of cultured art he set the values of rebellion and dissidence, the sole guarantors of true creativity, as embodied by the originators of what Dubuffet termed 'Art Brut'. In order to recapture the capacity for wonder and a state of innocence before the canvas, Dubuffet attempted, in one picture after another, to invent anew the means he used, and to think up new procedures for creation. The Saint-Etienne collection does not include any work from the artist's earlier periods; none the less, it does give a good account of the astonishing diversity and prodigious inventiveness of his

Pierre Soulages (Rodez 1919)
Painting 19.6.79, 1979
Oil on canvas; 220 x 175
Purchased, 1982. Inv. 82.7.1

73

Jean Dubuffet
Le Havre 1901 - Paris 1985
Site avec deux personnages, E 290, 1981
Acrylic on paper mounted on canvas;
50.5 x 68. Deposited by the National
Museum of Modern Art, 1988

Jean Dubuffet
Le Havre 1901 - Paris 1985
Illusory Site, 1963
Oil on canvas; 195 x 130
Purchased, 1984. Inv. 84.6.1

oeuvre. Ranging in content from the 1958 *Texturology XLVII* to the 1984 *Non Lieu,* the collection includes a number of major works illustrating the most important phases of the second half of his career. *Texturology XLVII – Innate Life* (1958) belongs to one of the most austere series of works figuring in the artist's abundant production. Following the unbridled, 'childish' figurations which had caused outrage and at the same time established his reputation, the artist appears here to be evolving towards a type of 'abstract' painting made up of projections encircled by droplets, thus forming an 'all over' space recalling Pollock. These paintings are, in fact, representational works evoking the texture of various types of soil. They show that Dubuffet's true concern is not always the spectacular and grandiose, but rather the small-scale, the tiny, the minuscule, that which is undifferentiated—everything that is all too hastily decreed to be 'trivial', yet which, at a very fundamental level, makes up our world.

It was Dubuffet's exploitation of minor coincidence that led to the birth of the extensive *Hourloupe* cycle of paintings. The starting-point for these was a number of red and blue ballpoint drawings which Dubuffet had sketched mechanically during telephone conversations. *Illusory Site* (1962) is one of the most complex works of the early years of the *Hourloupe* cycle. In it, the potentialities of these tiny improvised schematic drawings are elaborated, being extended and multiplied, and their evocative power and capacity to structure are brought out. When the *Hourloupe* cycle came to a halt, its creator seems to have felt the need to engage in a kind of

stock-taking: the 'théâtres de mémoire' (*The Decoder*, 1977), which are huge collages of cut-out, individually painted fragments, bring together, in the form of 'quotations', the periods and styles of previous works. The clashes of irregular contours and the chaos that results from the mixture of so many heterogeneous styles are in fact transcended through the use of a single unifying technique. The result, at once contradictory and coherent, is a mirror of Dubuffet's whole subver-

Jean Dubuffet
Le Havre 1901 - Paris 1985
The Decoder, 1977
Acrylic on cut-out paper glued to canvas
(28 assembled pieces); 178 x 214
Purchased, 1984. Inv. 84.7.1

sive oeuvre. In 1980-81, forced by ill-health to work sitting down, Dubuffet completed a series of small-format compositions—*Psychosites*—in which small, simplified figures are set against backgrounds depicting indistinct, erratic, indecipherable locations. These same uncertain, breathless, nervously executed expanses were later the subject matter of the *Mire* series (*Mire*, 1983).   J.B.

Chaissac, Michaux, Fautrier, Richier

Although he had taken part in some of the events staged by the Art Brut movement, Chaissac later denied any kind of

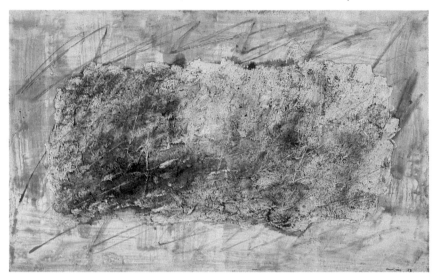

Gaston Chaissac
Avallon 1910 - La-Roche-sur-Yon 1964
Totem, 1964
Enamel paint on wood; 59 x 25.8 x 6
Donated by the Friends of the Museum,
1966. Inv. 66.1.1

Jean Fautrier
Paris 1898 - Châtenay-Malabry 1964
Broken Lines, 1958
Oil on paper glued to canvas; 73 x 116
Purchase, 1982. Inv. 82.20.1

Henri Michaux
Namur 1899 - Paris 1984
Untitled, *c.* 1956
Watercolour on rice paper; 47 x 62
Marcel Boussac Donation, 1958
Inv. 58.7.1

membership of this new artistic category invented by Dubuffet. His background was a humble one, and, though entirely self-taught, he owes his vocation as a painter to artists such as Otto Freundlich and Albert Gleizes, who inspired him to paint. Chaissac's art is not reducible to any established aesthetic; it is the art of an eternal rebel. He refused to conform to fashion, remained indifferent to commercial considerations, and stayed far away from the great centres of the art

76

world, letting his creative energy busy itself spreading enamel paint on unexpected supports (stumps of wood, odd pieces of detritus, crushed leaching-machines), which he used as catalysts for his imagination (*Totem*, 1962). Open to every suggestion, to every means of expression, he was willing even to include writing in his work. In this respect he is comparable to Michaux, the reverse, 'cultured' side, as it were, of a philosophy that led them both to envisage art as a synthetic process. Michaux concentrated on drawing and watercolour, because of their proximity to writing and because of their unpredictable nature. He used automatism (sometimes stimulated by drugs) as a way of arriving at the essence of the individual self, of recapturing a measure of primary starkness (*Untitled*, c. 1956).

The war, with its charnel houses and massacres, brought with it a similar tragic, stark exposure of the human condition for Fautrier. This dire experience made him want to reinvent painting, to find new methods for it, and new meanings. Starting from raw, formless 'primary' material, he managed, through an intense process of kneading, grinding, and scratching, precisely to *inform* the material, to restore meaning to it (*Broken Lines*, 1958).

This same existential anguish is documented in the art of Réquichot (who committed suicide at 32). His remarkable body of work is shot through with the notions of confinement, contradiction, and decomposition. These ideas persist right up to the last great collages, in which everyday images cut out of magazines lose their individual meaning and intelligibility and are reconstituted into an 'abstract' network of organic forms, an improbable world of interlocking cells (*Vibroskomenopatof*, 1960).

Germaine Richier was one of the originators, with Alberto Giacometti, of the new expressionist style that is now regarded as best illustrating the post-war period. Executed shortly after the war, the *Mantis* seems still haunted by the fears of that period, providing a concentrated expression of them. The piece is one of a group of sculptures which depict animals, the elements, and nature in its wild state, and in so doing take us back to the origins of humanity, reimmersing us in a world dominated by the anguish of early man. Coming as it does hard on the heels of the war, the *Mantis* bears witness to the crisis in humanistic values and to the doubt concerning man's ability to control his destiny. The rough, nervous, tense style created by Germaine Richier gives expression to this deep-seated anxiety, and to the utter confusion experienced by the individual whose very humanity is under threat.

J.B.

Germaine Richier
Grans (Bouches-du-Rhône) 1904 - Paris 1959
The Mantis, 1946
Bronze; 66.5 x 26 x 27
Anonymous gift, 1990

The 1960s and 1970s

1960 established itself as one of the crucial dates of the twentieth century. Even though no significant events are recorded for that opening year of the decade, it none the less 'symbolizes' the Kennedy era, the Americanization of the West, the growth of the consumer society, and so on. In France, Pierre Restany's *Manifeste du Nouveau Réalisme* grouped together, and thus shed new light on, a number of works which for some years had run counter to the aesthetic trends under which they were classified. A similar situation had emerged in the United States, where the works of Rauschenberg and Johns were beginning to be viewed as outside the action-painting ethic. In both Paris and New York, at what seemed to be a time of triumph for geometric abstraction and Abstract Expressionism, two trends emerged: on the one hand, a resumption of links with Dada, with pride of place accorded to objects; and, on the other, a figurative bent exploiting what photography, film, and advertising had to offer. In both cases, what was rejected was the display of paradigmatic uniqueness associated with styles of artists 'of genius'; and what was aimed at was the preservation of the artist's anonymity. The latter saw himself either as an art-producing machine designed to subvert the society that consumed him, or else as a sociologist, criticizing all artistic production sanctioned by the ruling classes. As a result, the 1960s saw the emergence of 'cold' artistic ideas and practices, giving precedence to the 'validity' of theory over the creation of the work of art. This trend had its roots in a particular interpretation of the work and attitude of Duchamp, as well as in Constructivism—then undergoing rediscovery—and a reductionist and mechanistic interpretation of painting (couched in Marxist and Freudian terms).

Nouveau Réalisme could provide us with an inventory of the objects typifying urban society as it made the transition from the industrial age to the post-industrial era of consumerism and communication. In this connection, however, Yves Klein's approach is not without some ambiguity, spread-angled as it is between a mystic quest for the absolute and the act of mystification accomplished by transmuting air and empty space into 'gold'. Pop Art supplies us with the icons of this transitional age, in the form of its 'emblematic' cans of soup, packets of washing powder, and snatches of comic-strip, handled in accordance with the reproductive techniques of those most common of media, the comic-strip and the advertisement, but simplified in a manner recalling the great works of

Foreground: Donald Judd, *Untitled*, 1989. Light and black anodized aluminium; 99, 5 x 199 x 199. Purchased, 1990.
Background (left to right): Donald Judd, *Progression*, 1972; Tom Wesselmann, *Illuminated Still Life*, 1964; On Kawara, *Mar. 14* and *Apr. 04, 1978*; Ellsworth Kelly, *Blue Panel*, 1988.

Arman, Armand Fernandez, known as
(Nice 1928)
Accumulation of Loudspeakers, 1963
Radio loudspeakers, wooden box;
122 x 63
Purchased, 1982. Inv. 82.14.1

Matisse. In a parallel development, the work of art was being reduced to primary forms and structures, both brutal in their simplicity and complex in their significance—if one accepts the postulate that they are the source of all constructed forms. And of course there were the investigations, under the aegis of topology, into the paradigms of antiform. Then, as if this attempt at classification seemed somehow perverted by the actual work itself, artists began to posit the reduction of the work to its concept, which merely required enunciation. Paradoxically, it was via this route that the subject, with its delight in introspection and its affirmation of ego, was re-introduced. The stumbling-block of dandyism is only just avoided in the taxonomical 'methodologies' of the time—irksome parodies of the social sciences, which then reigned supreme and were far too inclined to overrate themselves in their attempt to furnish general interpretations of particular acts and creations. These sciences provided the justification for the recourse to 'action'—derived from the 'happening', from Futurist events, and from Dada—which it was possible, not long after this, to record on video. In these works, the body becomes the principal player. Towards the end of the decade, art seemed to condense into attitude. These were the basic tenets on which the 1970s survived, though at the start of the decade the radical turn taken by Buren, Toroni, Mosset, and Parmentier heralded a return to the actual work of art: a theory is stated, but the work itself is no longer reduced to mere concept of posture—its physical reality is affirmed. The practitioners of Support(s)/Surface(s)—particularly those who had deliberately opted to work away from the capital—embraced this trend with confidence. Their apparent deconstruction of the mechanics of paintings went beyond a functionalist dismantling aimed at 'Taylorizing' artistic production; it rapidly assumed 'primitivist' overtones. What results is akin in form to post-minimalist work, and in concept to Arte Povera; from the point of view of theory, however, it seems reminiscent of the questioning of art also engaged in by Polke and Richter, though these focused more on image and representation, producing that familiar rigour and grandeur. At the start of the 1980s, it was the work of these artists that engaged attention. What was 'commendable' about their attitude—to parody André Chastel—was that it sprang from the momentary. What had been masked throughout the 1970s by the totalitarian classicism of avant-garde trends now became visible. The expressive, 'baroque' exhilaration that celebrates the work of art restored the artist to his mission as creator. The actual painting or sculpture—evidence of a 'new spirit' in art—established precedence over mere attitude, and the masterpiece regained its supremacy over serial production.   B.C.

Nouveau Réalisme At the end of the 1950s and beginning of the 1960s, important changes began to affect society, as it turned increasingly towards mass consumption and the organization of leisure and leisure activities. Art, for its part, professed realism and—a trend favoured by the times—newness. Reality, dominated by the production of objects, began to claim the attention of artists, who made it the focal point of their creative activities.

The keynote of Arman's accumulations is quantity—that feature so typical of the times. With his piles of objects—in this case loudspeakers—the artist punctuates space in a kind of obsessive repetitiveness. The nature of the object is no longer revealed through its uniqueness but through its multiplicity. Moreover, the deterioration which an object may suffer cannot halt the process of 'revelation', as witnessed by *Studio Dustbin* (1964), similar in form to certain gestural works

Daniel Spoerri (Galati, Romania, 1930)
Throw Out the Baby with the Bath Water,
1967
Assemblage of objects on plywood;
150 x 95
Purchased, 1983. Inv. 83.12.2

Arman, Armand Fernandez, known as
(Nice 1928)
Studio Dustbin, 1964
Various objects and items of rubbish in
cardboard box screwed to panel;
122 x 100 x 29.5
Purchased, 1983
Inv. 83.12.1A

belonging to the previous generation and which Arman here takes to task in a manner not unreminiscent of the derisive attitude of Dada.

Just as opposites ultimately encounter one another and are transformed, so Arman's proliferation becomes César's compression. The car, once a cult object of the Futurists and a means for them of extolling the true pace of civilization, is transformed, in César's work, into a locus of concentrated, almost petrified energy.

Daniel Spoerri displays the meticulously disciplined approach of the entomologist as he turns the spotlight on, and at the same time discloses the nature of, ordinary everyday objects brought together by chance. This essentially poetic gesture highlights the possibilities latent in everyday existence, and the use of ordinary language to express that existence brings out its full flavour. Thus *Throw Out the Baby with the Bath Water*, a veritable visual proverb, is a fine example of the richness that results from the interplay of word and object.

A similar taste for manipulating word and form is evident in the derivative practices of Raymond Hains, Jacques de la Villeglé, and François Dufrêne. The torn posters which are the focus of their attention are removed—either in whole or in part—from the wall and glued, just as they are, on to canvas, or else left on their zinc supports. Thus a deformed object is

Jacques de la Villeglé (Quimper 1926)
Crossroad Beaubourg-Rambuteau, 1972
Torn posters glued to canvas; 182 x 246
Deposit from the Martine and Didier
Guichard Collection

removed from its usual context, takes on a new form, and can subsequently be looked at, not for its commercial or political message, but rather for the imbroglio of forms, rhythms, and colours produced by the successive layers of posters.

In Martial Raysse the eye no longer derives its pleasure from that chance confrontation of unconnected objects which produces the poetic shock beloved of Surrealists. Instead, visual enjoyment results from the integration of everyday objects into a process of global 'poeticization'. Thus the new plastic utensil, the photograph of a woman, the modern setting with its flashing neon lights become objects of a fascination that is made possible only by a clinical vision disencumbered of the

Raymond Hains (Saint-Brieuc 1926)
Three Panels from the Sidney Jeanine Period,
1960
Torn poster on sheet metal; 210 x 310
Deposit from the Martine and Didier
Guichard Collection

Martial Raysse (Golfe-Juan 1936)
Hygiene of Vision, Double Portrait, 1968
Painted metal and plywood with
silk-screen print on torchon paper;
200 x 110 x 30
Deposited by the FNAC, 1989

Yves Klein
Nice 1928 - Paris 1962
Monochrome IKB, 1957
Paint on canvas glued to hardboard;
50 x 50 x 5.5
Purchased, 1973. Inv. 73.8.1

dross of habit. Yves Klein is probably the most legendary of the protagonists of Nouveau Réalisme, even though his work is, in fact, somewhat removed from that of the other artists who signed the movement's manifesto in 1960. His monochrome works, and in particular the famous International Klein Blue, appear as manifestations of pure feeling, a goal which the artist was constantly seeking to attain and which he wanted the whole world to enjoy. Klein's blue was a universal ethical response to a society which, he believed, was too inclined to materialism. The whole of Klein's work is imbued with a certain esoteric spirituality, but there has been a tendency to overplay this. Nevertheless, it remains true that Klein's objective was to bring about—through art and in art—the advent of a new era, in which harmony of forms and of life-styles would finally be achieved.   M.F.

Pop Art
As early as 1973, the Museum managed to enhance its collection with a highly representative set of works from American Pop Art. Andy Warhol is probably the artist who best embodies the American school of the sixties. The outcry prompted by his exhibitions, his manner, his entourage, his whole personality, fostered the emergence of a new status for the artist. For Warhol, that obsessed despiser of images, the triumph was emphatic. The haunting, ubiquitous icons of contemporary photography, advertising, and cinema were increasingly losing their emotional and symbolic value. Taking up the challenge, as it were, Warhol set about levelling them out completely. Using a technique well suited to the task (acrylic-based serigraphy) and fashionable colours, he produced a whole series of depictions of these stereotyped

images of American culture. From tins of Campbell's Soup to Elvis Presley, from electric chairs to car crashes, from Coca-Cola bottles to self-portraits, the images emerge one after another, coldly and mechanically reproduced on the canvas. *Self-Portrait* of 1966 is one of this number. The two dominant colours, applied in large flat areas, and the forms themselves, produced using the techniques of photography, accentuate the loss of meaning. This canvas is, incidentally, dedicated to Nico, female vocalist with the rock group Velvet Underground, of which Warhol was the producer. *Diamond Dust Shoes* belongs to the later style. The seductive quality of the

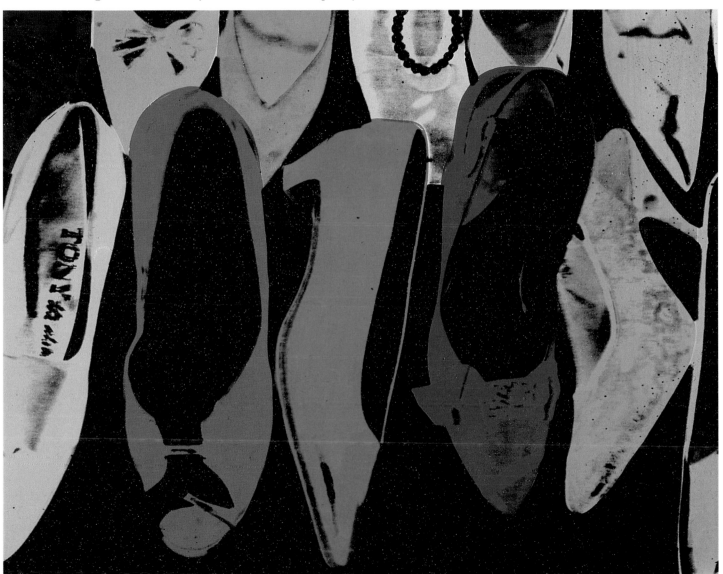

picture—achieved mainly by the use of diamond-like spangles—shares the same illusory character.

In Tom Wesselmann's *Illuminated Still Life* there is also a reference to the standardized image, as it appears in the streets of big cities. The plastic box, with its paint applied using the industrial methods of the sign-writer, reinforces the coldness of the image, without, however, robbing it of any of its power of attraction. Wesselmann is a master at exploiting the ambivalence of contemporary stereotypes. But the questions he poses are not confined to the sociological: they also encom-

Andy Warhol
Pittsburgh 1930 - New York 1987
Diamond Dust Shoes, 1980
Acrylic and silk-screen with diamond dust on canvas; 178 x 229
Deposit from the Martine and Didier Guichard Collection

Tom Wesselmann (Cincinnati 1931)
Illuminated Still Life, 1964
Moulded plexiglass, electric light;
122 x 152
Purchased, 1973. Inv. 73.5.3

Andy Warhol
Pittsburgh 1930 - New York 1987
Self-Portrait, 1966
Oil (serigraphic transfer) on canvas;
57 x 57
Purchased, 1973. Inv. 73.5.2

Jim Dine (Cincinnati 1935)
Putney Winter Heart (Crazy Leon), 1971-72
Acrylic on canvas and objects; 186 x 186
Purchased, 1973. Inv. 73.5.1

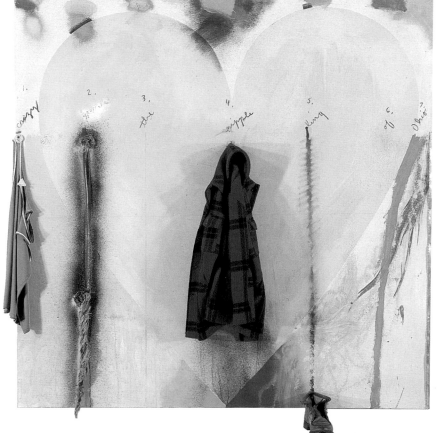

pass art and the history of art. This is demonstrated here by the implicit reference to two great masters of the twentieth century: Mondrian, from whom Wesselmann borrows the right-angles grids and chromatic ranges; and Matisse—as exemplified in the *Large Pink Nude*—from whom he adopts strict composition and purity of form.

Entablature, which follows on from Roy Lichtenstein's enlarged comic-strips of the early sixties, is part of a series of works in which the artist also pursues his questioning of painting and of the history of art in general. Though many of Lichtenstein's images are direct quotations, his repetition of

motifs and neutral technique produce an effect of critical distancing. The horizontal lines in *Entablature* start off as details of the façade of a Greek temple but go on subtly to recall the composition of certain works by Minimalist artists such as Kenneth Noland and Donald Judd.

The work of Jim Dine occupies a position on the periphery of American Pop Art. The inclusion of real objects in his canvases does, it is true, recall the work of Wesselmann, but in Wesselmann the objects are new, straight off the conveyor belt, whereas in Dine they show signs of wear and tear. The objects are often drawn from the immediate context in which the artist lives. The execution is not smooth and regular but recalls the abstract gestural painting of the previous generation. And, whereas Pop Artists are painting the external landscape, Dine, as he himself has acknowledged, tends rather to a depiction of interior scenery. M.F.

Roy Lichtenstein (New York 1923)
Entablature, 1974
Magna and metallic paint on canvas;
178 x 284.5
Purchased, 1987. Inv. 87.8.1

Bernard Rancillac (Paris 1931)
The Last Whisky, 1966
Vinyl paint on canvas; 225 x 200
Purchased, 1986. Inv. 86.10.1

Figuration Narrative

The main feature that distinguished the art of the 1960s, as a whole, from previous trends was a clear return to figure and narrative. In France in the middle of the decade, the Figuration Narrative movement, whose compositions owe much to the language of the media, reverted to a style of art with content, in which ideology and political commitment often feature.

Thus Bernard Rancillac's offering to art takes the form of comic-strip heroes. In his earlier style, illustrated in the Museum's collection by *The Dance of the Starveling* of 1965, the figures burst on the scene in a vehement canvas characterized by evocative forms and loud colours. In *Last Whisky* the composition is more sober, and the near-perfect image ensnares us. The forms are faultless, the colouring is powerful and clear, there is an atmosphere of nostalgia: the picture is totally persuasive. This same persuasiveness is no doubt also the goal in the political paintings of the artist's next period. These are huge instructional frescos in which Maoist ideology also strives to appear attractive.

This conception of art is shared by Hervé Télémaque. Using a rather more subtle approach and a language that embraces the plastic techniques of Surrealism, he produces a canvas—

Convergence—condemning the treatment of Blacks in an America still dominated by apartheid.

Jacques Monory's subject matter is not so much political violence as the insidious violence of everyday life. Each of his canvases tells a story, in which the scenes of murder and the encounters charged with consequences allude to the artist's own life or to personal fantasies. The incidents are literally staged, using cinema techniques, and they always convey an impression of distance; the almost exclusive use of blue accentuates this and prolongs the feeling of anguish created by the anonymity of the locations.

Violence is also a feature of Gilles Aillaud's work, but is not treated, as it is by the previous artists, in a demonstrative way. In the zoo scenes painted in great number by the artist, it remains latent. His is the theme of confinement *par excellence*,

Jacques Monory (Paris 1934)
Murder No. 1, 1968
Oil on canvas; 162.5 x 391
Deposited by FRAC Rhône-Alpes, 1984

Hervé Télémaque (Port-au-Prince 1937)
Convergence, 1966-67
Acrylic, collage, and objects on canvas;
two canvases separated by a
skipping-rope; in total: 195 x 260
Purchased, 1982. Inv. 82.15.1

Gilles Aillaud (Paris 1928)
Hippopotamus II, 1975
Oil on canvas; 130 x 162
Purchased, 1979. Inv. 79.31.1

Alain Jacquet (Neuilly 1939)
Gaby d'Estrées, 1965
Serigraphic transfer on canvas; 119 x 172
Purchased, 1974. Inv. 74.2.1

but his paintings go beyond straightforward narrative; they make use of exploratory techniques characteristic not so much of a manipulator of images as of an organizer of forms. Alain Jacquet, for his part, undertakes a critical observation of the notion of the work of art. His use of image, through the intermediary of borrowed works of art, produces a kind of questioning of the traditional characteristics of artistic subject matter. With *Gaby d'Estrées*, a canvas mechanically duplicated several dozen times, the artsit offers us an intentionally modernist version of the famous painting of the Fontainebleau School, at the same time playing havoc with the laws of the market by breaking the normal rule of uniqueness for works of art.

Although not directly linked to the Figuration Narrative movement—because in many cases they preceded it—the works of Bettencourt, Dado, and even of Baj adhere to a con-

Enrico Baj (Milan 1924)
Dama (Lady Elisabeth Bruce), 1963
Assemblage and oil on furnishing
fabric; 92 x 73
Purchased, 1964. Inv. 64.20.1

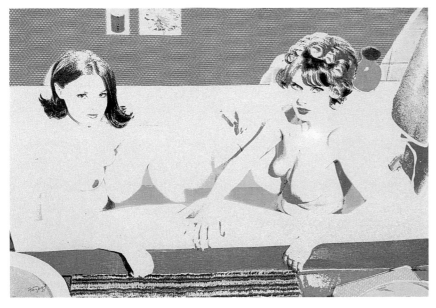

ception of art in which pictorial data cannot blunt content. Thus Enrico Baj's *Dama (Lady Elisabeth Bruce)* typifies a period in which the physical material—in this case glued-on trimmings—is used to create ironic baroque settings where 'portraits' of the generals and great ladies of history occupy pride of place.

Also situated rather more on the fringe, the work of Peter Stämpfli is little concerned with narrative, and remains distant from the spirit of Pop Art, even though its subject matter—the car and, soon after, the single tyre—does allow some comparison. The constant repetition of the subject justifies us

Peter Stämpfli (Deisswil, Switzerl., 1937)
Rallye, 1964
Oil on canvas; 173 x 188
Purchased, 1979. Inv. 79.38.1

in thinking that what we have here is not merely a reflection on pure painting and the plastic product, but that the artist has clearly invested himself in the picture, in the same way as Jean-Pierre Raynaud does, though in a less fraught manner. In Raynaud, the artist's investment of himself often also assumes a tragic dimension: death, madness, confinement in an enclosed space are constant features of the early works. *Zero Space* is both a summary of these themes and an attempt to move beyond them.   J.B.

Minimal Art The origins of Minimal Art are to be sought in the type of painting described by Clement Greenberg as 'Post-Painterly Abstraction'—notably the 'colourfield' developed by Louis and Noland—and also, and primarily, in the work of two major artists: Ellsworth Kelly and Frank Stella. Even before 1960, Kelly and Stella had established a new vision of painting, the effects of which depended essentially on the conditions attending the perception—immediate perception—of a 'non-relational', non-hierarchized space. In his 'black paintings', Stella had sought to make this space perfectly homogeneous by creating a series of compositions where the simple, elementary motifs were organized according to a 'deductive structure' that influenced, or rather determined, even the shape of the canvas (hence the 'shaped canvas'). *Agbatana II* (1968) belongs to the important 'protractor' series, a set of variations based on the shifts in position of a protractor. The overall scheme of configurations, determined as early as 1967, puts a *de facto* prohibition on any kind of deviation or excess of subjectivity. The series is made up of a group of thirty-one different configurations, each of which acts as a base for three types of motifs, assigned by Stella to the categories 'interlace', 'rainbow', and 'fan'. Each canvas bears a title alluding to the circular plans of the ancient cities of Asia Minor. The polished execution and the use of cool, flat, fluorescent acrylics sanction the disappearance of style. *Parczezew* (1971), with its interplay of divergent tensions and its clashes of material, heralds the 'baroque' course taken by Stella's work during the 1980s.

In his *Two Panels: Blue-Yellow* (1970), Kelly, who studied in Paris, seems still under the influence of Matisse's paper cutouts. Applied flat across two separate supports that are simply abutted, the colour is perfectly homogeneous, its autonomy respected. The quality of each of the colours, applied in subtle measure, is dependent on its proximity to the other colour and on considerations related to strictly material notions of extent and quantity. In *Blue Panel* (1988), the use of monochrome adapted to the shaped canvas shifts attention to the edges of the painting, which, more than ever, finds its meaning in the relationship which it sets up with the space that contains it. In contrast to Stella and Kelly, Kenneth Noland has always acknowledged a certain measure of independence for colour, compared to his approach to problems of size and shape. The 'horizontal stripe' series, to which *Clearing* (1967) belongs, is one of the most coherent works

from this point of view. Noland here exploits the chromatic possibilities of bands of colour set in canvases of narrow, elongated, horizontal format, of which they are, as it were, the echo.

Rejecting the geometric approach, Larry Poons attempts, in canvases that are like 'matterist' versions of Morris Louis' 'veils' (*Leavening*, 1975), to give colour back its weight and

Frank Stella (Malden, USA, 1936)
Agbatana II, 1968
Acrylic on canvas; 280 x 457
Purchased, 1973. Inv. 73.1.1

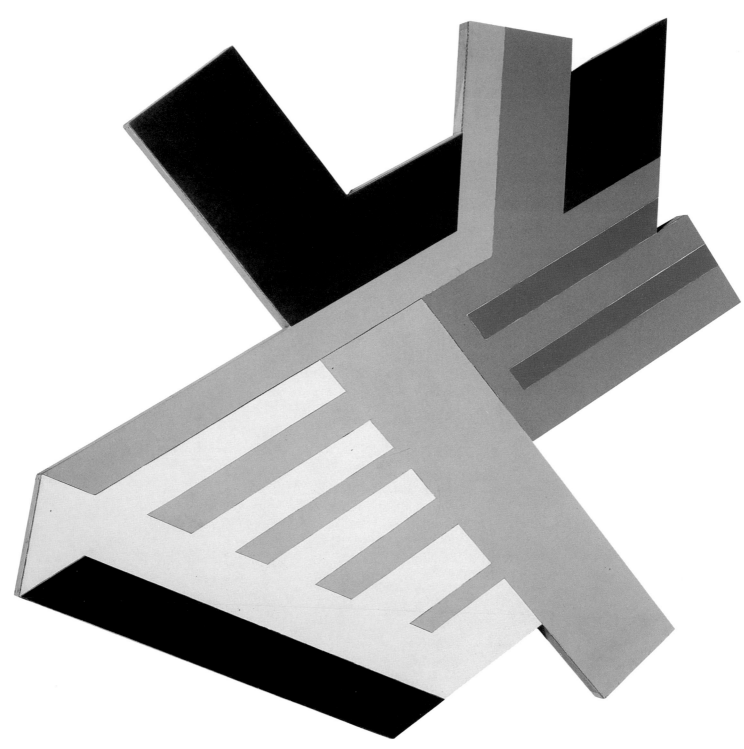

Frank Stella (Malden, USA, 1936)
Parczezew, 1971
Canvas, felt on cardboard, on wood;
290 x 280 x 10
Purchased, 1986. Inv. 86.12.1

Ellsworth Kelly (Newburgh, USA, 1923)
Blue Panel, 1988
Oil on canvas; 97 x 340
Purchased, 1988. Inv. 88.11.1

Elsworth Kelly (Newburgh, USA, 1923)
Two Panels: Blue-Yellow, 1970
Acrylic on canvas; two panels joined:
77.5 x 210 (each), 77.5 x 420 (together)
Purchased, 1989. Inv. 89.7.1

Kenneth Noland (Ashville, USA, 1924)
Clearing, 1967
Acrylic on canvas; 33 x 295
Purchased, 1975. Inv. 75.1.1

unfettered indeterminateness. An affirmation of the physical reality of the work of art, a rejection of illusionism, a taking into account of real space, clarity of operation—all these notions are to be found in the work of the Minimalist sculptors Judd, Morris, Flavin, Andre, and LeWitt. Their work—which claims to be operating, more so than painting, within real space—takes the form of stable, 'primary' structures with clean contours and surfaces, non-tactile, non-anecdotal, and created using standardized production methods. The artists hope in this way to shift the observer's eye from the work itself (which is no longer the locus of any action) towards the space that contains it, thus questioning its differential rela-

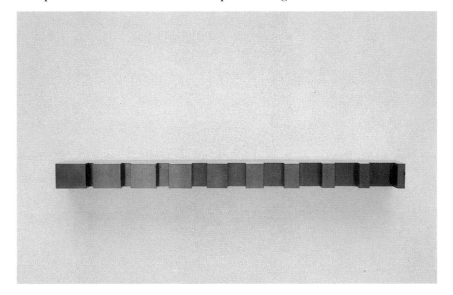

Donald Judd (Excelsior Springs, 1928)
Progression, 1972
Steel; 12.5 x 176 x 23
Purchased, 1973. Inv. 73.2.1

Carl Andre (Quincy, Mass., 1935)
Fin, 1983
Lead: 50 lead bricks; 20 x 10 x 5 (each)
20 x 500 x 5 (overall)
Purchased, 1985. Inv. 85.72.1

tionship to reality. According to Donald Judd, 'progressions' are a means of producing asymmetrical works that do not imply any composition. The lay-out of these mural sculptures is determined as a whole, according to a system, the order being dictated by various types of mathematical progression. The intervening spaces increase as the volumes decrease, with solids and spaces becoming equal units; the progression of the volumes echoes the inverse progression of the intervening spaces in a continuous toing and froing that determines the overall character of the piece.

Carl Andre's works, like Judd's, are conceived of as 'specific

Robert Morris (Kansas City 1931)
Felt Piece, 1974
Folded felt; extended: 190 x 970
Purchased, 1975. Inv. 75.2.1

objects' (Judd's term) and render the use of the plinth entirely superfluous. *Fin* (1983) is a repetition of standardized units, laid out on the ground, which recall the regular succession of 'modules' in Brancusi's *Endless Column*. But *Fin* is also a response to the Western tradition of upright, vertical sculpture still present in Brancusi's work.

Dan Flavin's work systematizes the use of the neon tube, a cold, technological material but at the same time a veritable condenser of energy. The *Monument for Vladimir Tatlin*, an explicit reference to the famous tower-shaped monument designed for the Third International, is indeed a tribute to the Soviet artist's Constructivist, Materialist ideas.

Sol LeWitt (Hartford, Conn., 1928)
Serial Project No. 1, A4, 1966
White-lacquered aluminium tubes,
3.7 cm-sided square section;
70.5 x 206 x 206
Deposited by FRAC Rhône-Alpes

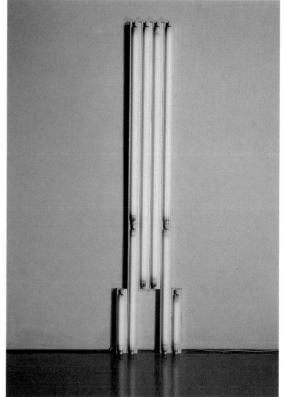

Dan Flavin, New York 1931
Monument for Vladimir Tatlin, 1975
Metal and neon tube; 304.5 x 61 x 12
Purchased, 1986. Inv. 86.13.1

Sol LeWitt (Hartford, Conn., 1928)
Untitled, 1966-68
Lacquered metal; 153 x 78 x 78
Purchased, 1973. Inv. 73.2.2

Having been one of the first to envisage sculpture in terms of 'primary structures', Robert Morris, concerned to give his work a dialectic form, also went on to become the pioneer, in the United States, of 'anti-form'. With his piles of earth or rubbish, and particularly with his cut-out or folded felt pieces (*Felt Piece*, 1974), he began a period of artistic reflection linking in with the problems of topology and perception which dominated his earlier work, and he analysed the potential qualities and indeterminable forms of materials in their raw or natural state. His approach marks him out from certain European artists such as Richard Long, whose wooden or

Barry Flanagan (Prestatyn, Britain, 1941)
Pile, 1968
Three folded pieces of coloured jute
canvas; approx. 18.5 x 57 x 46
Purchased, 1986. Inv. 86.18.1

Richard Long (Bristol 1945)
Winter Slate Line, 1985
Stones; 700 x 80
Purchased, 1985. Inv. 85.75.1

stone circles and lines (*Winter Slate Line*, 1985) perpetuate a romantic or archaic conception of landscape; it is more akin to the early works of Flanagan, whose *Piles* (1968) in coloured fabric suggest the possibility of a supple, aleatory, polychrome type of sculpture, opposed to the homogeneous, permanent forms of classical Western statuary.

Sol LeWitt's serial work takes the form of variations following on from the restricting choice made by the artist to use the square as his basic unit of vocabulary. He expounds and analyses all its potentialities, its combinations, every possible extrapolation and articulation (*Serial Project*, 1967).   J.B.

Conceptual Art
Sol LeWitt was probably the first to formulate the notion of Conceptual Art, described as a form of art in which the idea takes precedence over the material execution of the work. The latter, according to LeWitt, can only imply the adulteration of the original concept.

Thus in the view of Joseph Kosuth, who pushed modernist reductionism to even further limits than LeWitt, the meaning of art boils down to a proposition of tautological character, in which, as Claude Ginz has noted, 'the physical fact verifies the proposition and *vice versa*'. In *Five Words in Yellow Neon* (1965), the concrete reality of the work and the message it conveys coincide exactly, coalesce exactly, obviating any deviation in interpretation.

On Kawara (Kariya, Japan, 1932)
Mar. 14, 1978 and *Apr. 04, 1978*
Liquitex on canvas; 25.6 x 33.2
Purchased, 1986. Inv. 86.16.1 and 86.16.2

Joseph Kosuth (Toledo, Ohio, 1945)
Five Words in Yellow Neon, 1965
Yellow neon; 18 x 244
Purchased, 1979. Inv. 79.2.1

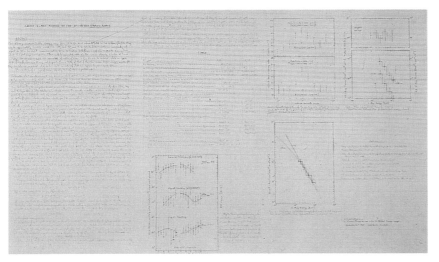

Bernar Venet (Saint-Auban 1941)
Cosmic X-ray Sources in the 20-180 kev Energy Range, 1967
Ink on graph paper mounted on panels; 100 x 173
Deposit from the Martine and Didier Guichard Collection

101

This same quest for unitary meaning leads Bernar Venet to include in his work objects, and later documents, that allow of only one level of interpretation—for example, mathematical diagrams, handwritten copies (*Cosmic X-ray Sources*, 1967) and later photographs and enlargements of passages from scientific works (*Introduction to the Theory of Categories and Functors*, 1970). To present the work of art as an established fact is also On Kawara's objective when, with no hint of 'psychologism', he reduces biographical content to a simple statement of the date, the only identifying factor provided (*Date Paintings*, 1978).

Sensation

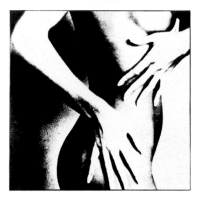

Create a little sensation
Feel the difference that everyone can see
Something you can touch
Property
There's nothing to touch it

ContraDiction

You've got it
You want to keep it
Naturally. That's conservation
It conserves those who can't have it
They don't want to be conserved
Logically, that's contradiction

Logic

Everything you buy says something about you
Some things you buy say more than you realise
One thing you buy says everything
Property
Either you have it or you don't

Victor Burgin (Sheffield 1941)
Sensation-Contradiction-Logic
Three photographic panels mounted on hardboard; each panel: 118 x 74
Purchased, 1982. Inv. 82.10.1

The compositions of the Art and Language Group and of Mel Ramsden (*Swift Reference Case*, 1971) are based on the belief that it is possible to extend the analytical models provided by linguistics to areas traditionally belonging to the plastic arts. Victor Burgin, closely linked to this group, has produced works which operate by establishing a link—it may be one of alienness—between text and image (*Sensation-Contradiction-Logic*, 1976), and he attempts in this way to endow the conceptual approach with a note of social criticism of the kind intrinsic to the intellectual climate of the time. J.B.

Support(s)/Surface(s)   The end of the 1960s was a time of creative ferment and questioning—even, and especially, in France, where American art, little known and little exhibited, was adopted as a model. To those artists who were to emerge as the avant-garde, it seemed that non-figurative art and the various forms of 'expressive' abstraction, with their overemphasis on 'the properties of the unique', had exhausted the potential of painting. As for Figuration Narrative, they regarded it as echoing the imagery of Socialist Realism and of geometric and kinetic abstractions that colluded with the smug complacency of a society that was losing its soul in

Olivier Mosset (Neuchâtel 1944)
Untitled, 1970
Oil on canvas; 100 x 100
Purchased, 1977. Inv. 77.18.1

Michel Parmentier (Paris 1938)
Untitled, 1968
Paint on unmounted canvas; 245 x 232.5
Purchased, 1977. Inv. 77.16.1

the rush to consumption. Only Nouveau Réalisme offered a way forward. Yet the succession of ready-mades which it presented were concerned not so much to overturn painting and sculpture but—in the wake of Duchamp—to assert the primacy of the concept of art; and its protagonists, fascinated by urban life, studiously avoided any analysis of the social function of art. This at least seems to have been the position of the artists who were to come to prominence in the various Support(s)/Surface(s) groups. Their first events were staged at about the same time as those of the BMPT group. Confronted, like Buren, Mosset, Parmentier, and Toroni, with issues relating to the social function of art, they attempted, not to downgrade the latter but rather to set it on a different course by gearing its own theory and practice to social theories and practices. Hence Bioulès, Dolla, Dezeuze, Saytour, Valensi on the one hand, and Pincemin, Cane, and Devade on the other, set about dismantling the mechanics of paintings, described as historically determined objects of know-

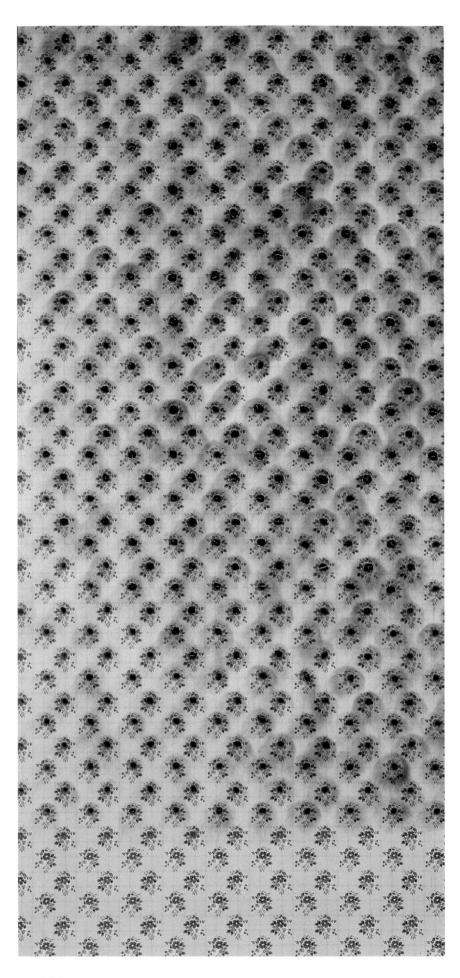

Patrick Saytour (Nice 1935)
Untitled, 1967
Printer, partially burned plastic material
mounted on panel; 300 x 136
Purchased, 1983. Inv. 83.16.1

Louis Cane
(Beaulieu sur Mer 1943)
Painting, 1972
Paint on cut-out canvas;
extended: 560 x 243
Purchased, 1973. Inv. 73.2.3

ledge, and analysing the operations proper to the exercise of painting.

Viallat summed up the thesis of the original protagonists of the group as follows: 'Dezeuze painted stretchers without canvases, I painted canvases without stretchers, and Saytour painted pictures of the stretcher on the canvas.' Fortunately, none of these artists' work can, in fact, be reduced to this kind of 'deconstruction' or specialization. The group of works by these artists housed in Saint-Etienne gives a clear picture of both the similarities and the radical differences between them. Thus in Valensi, Cane, Devade, and of course, Viallat, painting gives way to a process of dyeing in which support and surface coincide; the latter's material reality is affirmed in its reaction to the material reality of the pigment, which either impregnates just the surface, or penetrates deep into the fibre, or else spreads through the fabric by capillary action, depending on whether the canvas is fine or coarse, and depending on the fluidity of the pigment. The same attention to the physical properties of the material is to be found in Toni Grand, Bernard Pagès, and Daniel Dezeuze. Grand and Pagès dispensed with the plinth, the hallmark of Western sculpture, and set about literally exposing the operations involved in their work and the formal results that could be achieved with the material used. Thus Toni Grand—in the style of Robert Morris's work in felt—limits the sculptor's task to such activities as sawing beams along four-fifths of their length and inserting cross-pieces between the sections thus produced. The number of cross-pieces and the nature of the sawing determine the shape of the piece, which may be laid straight on to the floor or leant against a wall.

Pagès for his part sets up a contrast between the structure of corrugated iron and a collection of wooden sticks of various lengths, thus playing on the notion of the impossibility of reducing a natural object to the status of an artefact. Daniel Dezeuze marks the edges of sections of wood with veneer, in some cases stained, assembling them into simple grids, which may be displayed either extended across a wall or rolled out over the floor. The grid—that device developed during the fifteenth and sixteenth centuries as a means of capturing reality (and which has played a familiar and important role as a production structure in the twentieth century)—is here displayed in its application to the field of art. Bioulès also emphasizes edge and limit, not through staining but by covering the surface of the canvas with modulated brushstrokes, in a style that alludes to Matisse and Newman and depicts the work of every modern artist as determined by a 'progressive' flow of history and of the history of art. Marking and imprint are characteristic features of the work of Patrick Saytour and Claude Viallat. The floral motif repeatedly branded on to a piece of oilcloth in an almost uniform manner (everywhere except at the base of the work—perhaps in an allusion to Jasper Johns, as a way of identifying top and bottom of the piece) recalls both Klein and Toroni. But the true purpose of the work is an iconoclastic obliteration of the representational dimension that usually forms the chief constituent

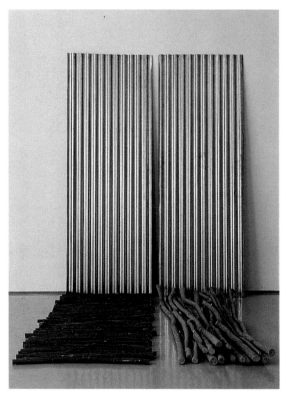

Bernard Pagès (Cahors, 1940)
Untitled, 1972
Two sheets of corrugated iron: 250 x 90
Sixty sticks stained red: 100 (approx.)
Sixteen sticks stained yellow: 275
(approx.)
Given by the artist, 1976. Inv. 76.12.1

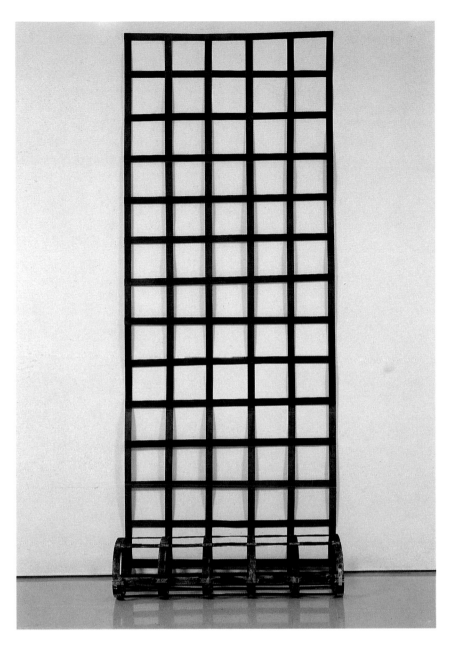

Daniel Dezeuze (Alès 1942)
Untitled, 1976
Thin sections of wood fastened and
stained; 112 x 950
Purchased, 1976. Inv. 77.1.1

Pierre Buraglio (Charenton 1939)
Window, 1975
Glass, wood, metal; 193 x 56.2
Purchased, 1989. Inv. 89.21.2

Claude Viallat (Nîmes 1936)
Le nœud du singe, c. 1970
Knotted ship's cable, knot stained with
walnut
Given by the artist, 1984. Inv. 84.11.1

107

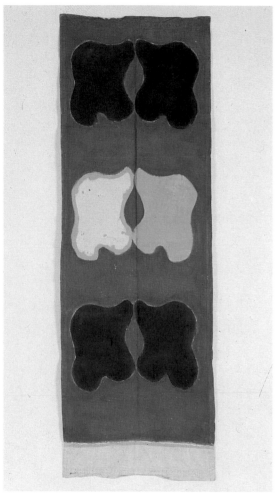

Claude Viallat (Nîmes 1936)
Painting, 1966
Casein on unmounted canvas; 190 x 62
Purchased, 1990

of a picture. The use of fire is evidence of the subversive intent typical of this generation; but it also demonstrates that a picture is the result of invention and of a procedure that can be explained by reference to history. In a similar vein, Viallat systematically repeats one supple shape—always the same size—across unfixed canvases; in contrast to stripes, bands, and brush-marks, this shape asserts itself through its sinuous contour and organic character, inviting comparison with Matisse's cut-out coloured shapes.

These artists, then, conceived painting within its means, as required by Viallat. And this led them logically to a broad consideration of the historical conditions governing the appreciation and 'exposition' of painting. Although the street events in which these artists engaged from 1966 to 1972 were also an affirmation of the reality of artistic objects, their main purpose was to integrate such objects into daily life, into natural space, outside the institutional framework in which painting is supposed to be shown. At the start of the 1970s, the artists' desire to co-ordinate theory and practice inevitably led them to advance a general interpretation of art, backed up by the social sciences, then very much in vogue. Thus they explained the irrational part of their art, their delight in colour, the pleasure they experienced in painting, and the pleasure of the observer by means of psychoanalysis. And, of course, their attempt at deconstruction was conceived of, historically, with the aid of Marxist philosophy, as interpreted at that time by Althusser and Balibar. Unfortunately, it was often for this theoretical contribution that they were extolled.

Nowadays works of art are taking the place of aesthetic-cum-political experiments. We are coming to realize that, like Robinson Crusoe, who survived the wrecking of a ship that symbolized civilization, these artists undertook to recreate art, but as Crusoe armed with a particular knowledge. Their aesthetic, in contrast to the modernist doctrines of the start of the century, did not aim to set out the framework of The Beautiful within which the ideal society might flourish; they sought instead to make the means by which painting was produced transparent to all—back to zero, enabling art to start off again from that point on a different, non-alienating route. No one at that time appreciated the romantic force of their purpose, similar in nature to that which motivated the exponents of Arte Povera.

We might say—recalling the title of a late 1960s exhibition—that the approach of these artists in fact embodied an anthropological interpretation of history which we now know to be indispensable.   B.C.

Arte Povera

In the mid-1960s, Italy witnessed the emergence of a movement—Arte Povera—which, though contemporaneous with American Minimal Art, sought, in contrast to the latter, to re-establish art on the basis of the senses by developing a veritable 'phenomenology of perception'. This poetic philosophy centres entirely on what a rediscovered Nature has to offer, including the products of the

Toni Grand (Gallargues 1935)
*Scantling, Partially Cut with Cross-Pieces in
Wood*, 1976; 500 x 40 x 14
Purchased, 1977. Inv. 77.24.1

Luciano Fabro (Turin 1936)
God's Eye, 1969
Wooden triangle and gilded wooden
rods; 180 x 180
Given by Michel Druand-Dessert, 1988
Inv. 88.12.1

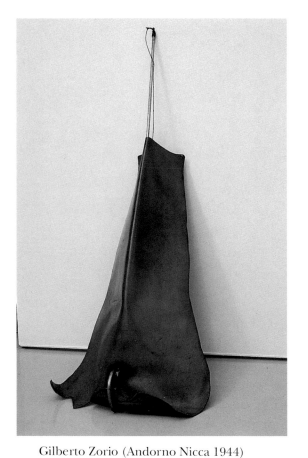

Gilberto Zorio (Andorno Nicca 1944)
Arco Voltaico, 1969
Leather and copper; 250 x 120 x 80
Purchased, 1985. Inv. 85.80.1

Giuseppe Penone (Garessio 1947)
Five-Metre Sapwood, 1973
Wood. Purchased, 1985. Inv. 85.79.1

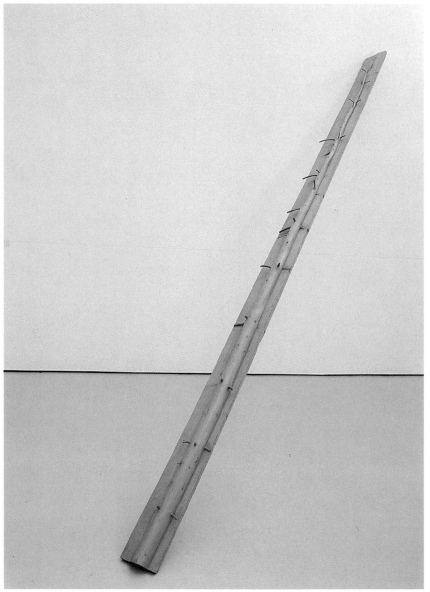

land. Thus use is made of a wide variety of materials—terracotta, leather, wool, glass, neon, steel—but also of perishable food-products such as fruit and vegetables; these are assembled by the artists into structures that almost always appeal to the prototypes of the world of the imagination. Materials and images that combine or clash rub shoulders in these compositions, in an interesting dialectical exchange. Mario Merz's work is precisely this kind of open yet closed location, where archetypal images—like his famous igloo—are once again given a voice. *Fibonacci Sequence* is made up of a triangular armature in rigid metal tubing, the oblique angles of

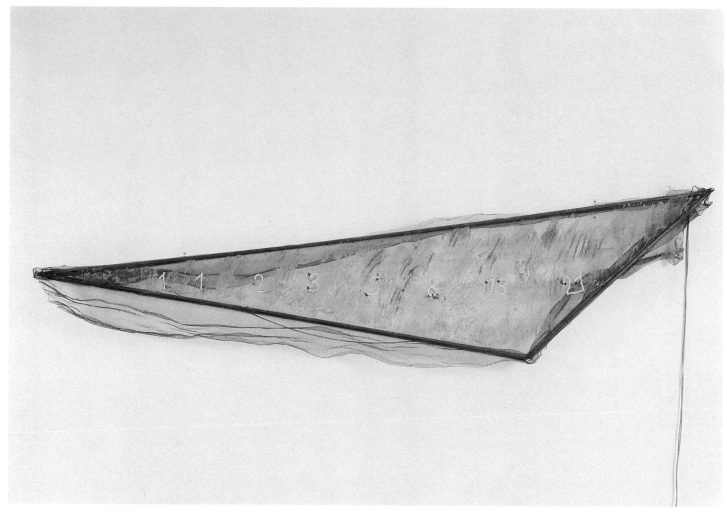

which recall the formal predilections of the Italian Futurists, and a flexible mesh, whose more random forms are reminiscent of the ubiquitous folds of baroque sculpture. But these historical references are not the only nods in the direction of time. The beeswax with which the artist coats the mesh, and the neon tube that takes up the idea of the numerical progression recorded by the Italian mathematician Fibonacci are both important symbols of temporality. Thus the numerical progression, whose acceleration symbolizes the spiral evolution of time, is countered by the timelessness of beeswax.

Time also figures in the work of Giuseppe Penone. *Five-Metre Sapwood* is a corroboration of Nature as a fundamental reference-point. In a subtle process of osmosis, the life of the individual is also written into the work: one can count off the

Mario Merz (Milan 1925)
Fibonacci Sequence, 1971
Neon, mesh, beeswax; 384 x 80 x 22
Purchased, 1985. Inv. 85.69.1

Christian Boltanski (Paris 1944)
Attempts at Reconstitution, 1970 and 1971
Five drawers in metal mesh, objects
modelled in plasticine;
each drawer: 40 x 60 x 13
Purchased, 1985 and 1989

years on the sapwood revealed by the sectioning of the trunk. Gilberto Zorio makes use of real materials—leather and copper—subjecting them to the effects of heat, which he also uses as a living material. This is Zorio's way of advancing a new philosophy of matter, in which the latter undergoes variations caused by ageing or other factors.

Experience is what underpins the work of Luciano Fabro: it claims our attention and appeals to the senses, here subjected to a process of re-education. *God's Eye* is an overt, not to say ostentatious, display of baroque techniques, applied here not without a degree of irony.

In the 1960s, at a time when activity in the psychoanalytic field was increasing and research into computers was beginning, time and memory became the emblematic themes of the works of many artists. These included Sarkis, Le Gac, and Boltanski, all of whom are represented in the Museum's collection, and each of whom, in his own way, casts an eye on this resurgence of the past and the memories it throws up. Given its fragile, volatile nature, memory is subjected to numerous attempts at preservation, as demonstrated by Sarkis in his 1974-76 composition *Piece*. Metal boxes, a museum display-case, long-playing records all seek to preserve or record, but—as the presence of weapons proves—the threat of total, final destruction remains.

Jean Le Gac's work is narrative in character, and its reduplications of images—often invaded by writing—form a kind of illusion of a personal diary, in which various biographical features, captions, quotations, and imprints repeatedly pose the question of artistic creativity and of its limits.

The objects formerly used by Christian Boltanski—and intimately connected with his childhood—are the subject matter of a rough plasticine copy, displayed in metal drawers covered in a flexible mesh. A wooden gun, a bowl, a notebook recall a past time which the artist attempts to recapture in the revelatory act of modelling. There is no doubt that the propensity to collect, order, label, and conserve is related to this laborious process of retention of the past, the ultimate derisory reflex-action in the face of a world where everything necessarily moves and progresses.   M.F.

German Painting
The defeat of Germany in 1945, the wish to expiate Nazism, and the introduction of the Marshall Plan all promoted the spread, in West Germany during the 1950s and 1960s, of an imported art—basically American in origin—and the disappearance of German art and of specifically German values. It was against this kind of cultural colonization and amnesia that a number of artists, chiefly from East Germany, took a stand, though they did not achieve international recognition (or even recognition within Germany) until the end of the 1970s. Thus Georg Baselitz, the content of whose paintings is a source of disquiet in the soothing context of consumer society, had several of his works simply banned. He was also one of the first to dare to display in his paintings certain 'Germanic' stylistic traits, in an attempt to end the long-standing repression of German

Sarkis (Istanbul 1938)
Untitled, 1974-76
Glass, discs, metal boxes, guns;
85.5 x 162.5 x 69.5
Given by the artist, 1976. Inv 76.8.1

Georg Baselitz
(Deutschbaselitz, Saxony, 1938)
Elke VI, 1976
Oil on canvas; 200 x 160
Purchased, 1982. Inv.82.3.1

A.R. Penck (Dresden 1939)
Meeting, 1976
Acrylic on canvas; 285 x 285
Purchased, 1982. Inv. 82.6.1

culture. Drawing on Expressionist sources, he countered the precise forms and clinical palette of Minimal and Pop Art with a brutal, fitful style, rendered even more baffling by his decision, in 1969, to execute his compositions upside down (*Elke VI*, 1976). Markus Lüpertz's powerful style of painting echoes that of Baselitz. For Lüpertz, painting is the expression of a kind of lyricism pushed to 'dithyrambic' heights, and 'dithyramb' is a term he often uses as a subtitle for his monumental compositions, frequently displayed in imposing serial arrangement (*Fassade-Stil*, 1977). Jörg Immendorf is another of the crucial figures on the Berlin scene. Berlin retained its status as a symbolic city, a place where separation

Markus Lüpertz (Liberec 1941)
Fassade-Stil, 1977
Oil and tempera on canvas; 250 x 183
Purchased, 1982. Inv. 82.2.1

Jörg Immendorf (Bleukede, GFR, 1945)
Café Deutschland. Schwarzer Stern, 1982
Oil on canvas; 282 x 400
Deposited by the FNAC. Inv. D.84.1.1

was a physical fact, and dispossession a daily experience. In the *Café Deutschland* series (*Schwarzer Stern*, 1982), Immendorf, in a style that still bears the hallmarks of his early, 'militant' art, presents us with a condensed picture of a Germany torn between opposing forces; the poetry of café life, the night, the glacial cold, national emblems, armoured vehicles all figure here. Penck, who took longer to reach the West, advertises contempt for the values of both East and West. Having left Dresden for Berlin, and later London, Penck found each of these cities an equal sham. Hence all his experimentation was aimed at developing a system of signs—executed in a direct synthesizing manner and borrowing equally from primitive civilizations and modern information-theory—geared to achieving immediate, universal communication (*Meeting*, 1976; *Incident in the Underground*, 1981).

J.B.

Gerhard Richter

The collection of works by Gerhard Richter housed in Saint-Etienne comprises six paintings and is thus the largest of its kind in France. It is to the traditional methods of teaching prevailing in East German art schools when he did the training in Dresden that Richter owes that technical ability which makes him an astonishing virtuoso, capable of mastering any style. His move to the West—to Düsseldorf—in 1961 led him, through the discovery of the Fluxus movement, of Beuys, and of 'happenings', to question the relationship between work and artistic activity. Although after his celebrated 'happening' entitled *Demonstration for Capitalist Realism* (1963) he made a return to painting, it would be a mistake to regard Richter's work as that of a 'painter'. His work springs from an analytical and critical attitude to painting, formulated using the means proper to painting, but deriving from an approach that is conceptual in nature. In Richter's view, 'painting has never painted anything but itself and nothing more' (Benjamin Buchloh). This is the key to Richter's constant changes of style, and his simultaneous use of opposing styles (*Glenn* and *Skull* were painted in the same year!). He believes that 'paintings must be constructed according to norms; the 'doing' has to take place without any participation of the inner self; the 'doing' is not an artistic act'. Whether applying grey paint (the only colour to 'manage not to represent anything') across the canvas (*Grey*, 1973); whether nonchalantly yoking together the three primary colours, with no particular thought for expression; whether painting highly connotational still lifes in ultimate *trompe-l'oeil* fashion (*Skull*; *Candle*, 1983); whether embarking on huge 'abstract' compositions that are in fact only simulations, representations of abstractions (*Glenn*, 1988)—what Richter is doing in each case is to pose anew the problem of the identity of painting.

J.B.

Gerhard Richter (Dresden 1936)
Skull, 1983
Oil on canvas; 95 x 90
Given by the artist and Liliane and
Michel Durand-Dessert 1984. Inv. 84.10.1

Gerhard Richter (Dresden 1936)
Vermalung, 1972
Oil on canvas; 200 x 200
Deposited by FRAC Rhône-Alpes

Gerhard Richter (Dresden 1936)
Glenn, 1983
Oil on canvas; 190 x 500
Purchased, 1984. Inv. 84.8.1

The 1980s

At the start of the 1980s, a new 'spirit' transported artistic activity away from the various 'classical' approaches that had characterized avant-garde art during the 1960s and 1970s. The beginnings of this unfolding of individualism had already become apparent in the preceding decade, particularly in Germany. Confronted simultaneously with the cultures of East and West, and with the historical and geographical reality resulting from the war, artists like Kiefer, Baselitz, Immendorf, and Penck regarded it as inconceivable that they should share the forward-looking values of avant-garde art, urging instead a search to recover a fundamental identity. Their apparent regression in fact expressed strong condemnation of dogmatic aesthetic viewpoints that sought to impose inviolable rules of modernity. Adherents of the Italian 'trans-avant-garde', whose links with historical events were not as close, demanded a similar freedom of individual decision, as did many French, English, and American artists. Schnabel, for example, like David Salle but in a different manner, ventures a few borrowings from classical painting, whilst asserting, in a style of baroque virtuosity and, in some cases, lavish effect, the heroic nature of the artistic epic. The links between Schnabel's work and the spirit of the avant-garde are evident, as they are in the work of Garouste. The latter's aesthetic has more in common—and the paradox here is merely apparent—with Marcel Duchamp than does that of the American simulationists. Although the work of these artists, with its display of scorn and celebration of 'kitsch' does offer a critical vision of art and society, it does not present us with a regenerative *tabula rasa*, nor with any revolutionary transformation of either. In view of this, it comes as no surprise to find many artists simulating classical or modern painting, and wandering around, not without a degree of nostalgia, in an 'imaginary' museum that has become a 'databank' from which to draw themes, forms, and motifs. Into this cosy world of contemporary art, however, graffiti artists and the heroes of Figuration Libre introduced the brutality of urban rock culture, as expounded by the 'tagger' and 'zapper'. Other attempted to restore to art the romantic, existential violence implied by having meaning and content—in short, they sought to restore 'a purer meaning' to accepted forms—for example, those of geometric art. Other artists again incorporated these forms into works presented as mobile objects, elusive 'ready-mades' whose semantic discrepancies are exploited via their ambiguous relationship to advertising.

John Armleder (Geneva 1948)
Untitled, 1986
Painted chair and platter; variable dimensions
Purchased, 1983. Inv. 87.2.1

Igor Kopystiansky (Lvov, Ukraine, 1954)
Interior, 1988
Oil on canvas and chairs;
195 x 288 x 295
Purchased, 1989. Inv. 89.25.2

David Diao (Chengdu, China, 1943)
Noise, 1988
Acrylic on canvas; 226 x 336.8
Purchased, 1989. Inv. 89.20.1

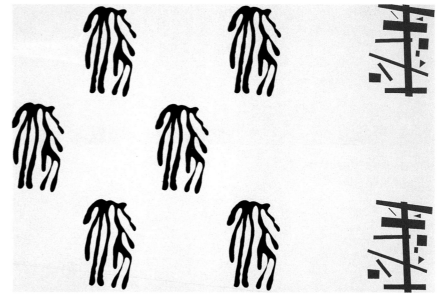

Philippe Favier (Saint-Etienne 1957)
Wind (Blue), 1986
Cold-worked enamel under glass;
15.5 x 23
Purchased, 1986. Inv. 86.11.2

Helmut Federle
(Solothurn, Switzerland, 1944)
Settlement Korea I, 1988
Acrylic on canvas; 230 x 330
Purchased, 1989. Inv. 89.26.1

After Modernism

The 1980s have often been described as ushering in the post-modernist age. They will be remembered as the period that witnessed the collapse of the avant-garde framework founded on a progressive notion of artistic activity, on the belief in a sort of absolute in art, a truth to whose essence every new, ever more 'radical' development was supposed to bring us closer. The 1980s marked the end of unitary theories; they were characterized instead by a burgeoning of experimental approaches—often contradictory—and by coexistence of antithetical artistic positions, given concrete shape in media (painting, video, photo-

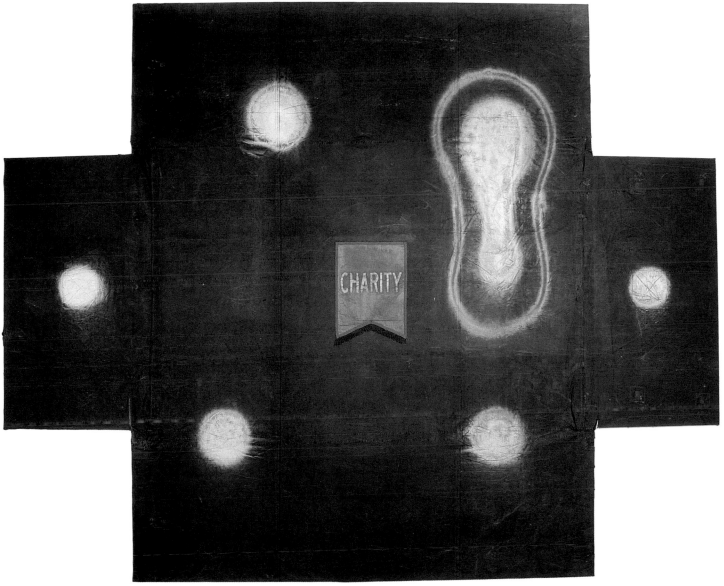

graphy, installations, objects, etc.) that also precluded exclusivity. The art of the 1980s belongs to the aesthetic of diversity described by certain historians as heralding, not the end of art, but the end of art as history (Hans Belting). For there is no way one could bring together into any ordered framework so many heterogeneous experiments: Julian Schnabel's powerful compositions, rich in content; the secret poetry of Philippe Favier's minuscule works; the quotation games of Diao and Kopystiansky, in which the history of art it-

Julian Schnabel (New York 1951)
Charity, 1986
Oil on canvas, sewn-on banner;
366 x 461.5
Purchased, 1987. Inv. 87.9.1

121

Harald Klingelhöller
(Mettmann, FRG, 1954)
Ich bin hier, Du bist hier, 1989
Cardboard and steel; 170 x 120 x 110
Purchased, 1990

Jochen Gerz, Berlin 1940
In the Art-Nite, 1989
Photographs; 460 x 790
Purchased, 1990

Bertrand Lavier
(Châtillon-sur-Seine 1949)
Relief Painting No. 1, 1988
Aluminium, enamelled sheet-metal,
glass; 250 x 500 x 10
Purchased, 1988. Inv. 88.10.1

Thomas Ruff (Zell, FRG, 1958)
Portrait, Christoph Steinmeyer, 1989
Cibachrome, plexiglass; 205 x 160
Purchased, 1990

Barbara Kruger (Newark, N.J., 1945)
*Promise Us Anything but Give Us
Nothing*, 1986
Photographs; three panels:
each 180 x 241
Purchased, 1987. Inv. 87.6.1

self becomes the subject of the painting: Cragg's transformation of objects; Armleder's or Lavier's 'simulationism', exploiting the ambiguities of everyday objects in order the better to question the meaning of the work of art, to grasp its true nature; the combination of the rigour of geometry and the uncertainty of colour in the intensely spiritual works of Federle; Perrodin's analytical approach; the critical conceptualism of Barbara Kruger's photographic panels; the refined verism of Jeff Wall's luminous Cibachromes; the manipulation of the self-portrait and consequent loss of identity in the scenes staged by Cindy Sherman ...   B.C.